My Life

Bobby Ball

Foreword by Tommy Cannon

Hodder & Stoughton
LONDON SYDNEY AUCKLAND

British Library Cataloguing in Publication Data

A record for this book is
available from the British Library

ISBN 0 340 64207 6

Printed and bound in Great Britain by
Cox & Wyman Ltd, Reading, Berks

Hodder and Stoughton Ltd
A Division of Hodder Headline PLC
338 Euston Road
London NW1 3BH

This book is dedicated to
my grandchildren

Contents

ILLUSTRATION ACKNOWLEDGMENTS

Cannon & Ball old, old, old: © Richard McLaren Photography

Bobby with Cannon and braces: © Richard McLaren Photography

Cannon, Ball and Eric Morecambe: © Studio G

Cannon & Ball with Gloria Hunniford: © London Weekend Television

Cannon & Ball with Prince Philip: © Thames Television

While every attempt has been made to trace the copyright holders of the photographs, the Publishers will be happy to rectify any missing acknowledgments in future editions.

Foreword

Fancy me, Tommy Cannon, writing a foreword about a book. Well, what can I say? Nothing! Because I have never written one before.

No, seriously, I know this will give me great pleasure to write, because it is about my partner and friend Bobby Ball.

Where do I start? Well, I suppose the best place to start is at the beginning. I first met Bobby at the Boden Trailers engineering factory in Oldham. I was the new boy standing by the clocking-in machine, when in came this little character and said, 'Hello, cock.' He was the first and only person to speak to me out of five hundred men. By the way, I make no excuses for the terminology of the word 'cock' because in Oldham it means pal or friend. And this friendship has lasted for thirty years.

To talk about Bobby before he became a Christian isn't easy. The moods he had at the time were unbearable. He found it difficult to talk to me about what was troubling him, so I in turn wouldn't talk to him. After several days I would go and say something daft to break the tension. I know a lot of it was to do with us becoming 'stars' (for the want of a better word) and the immense pressure that we were under. Also material things became more important than real life itself. Well, that's enough of the

past. He has now come out of the dark tunnel and into a
bright light.

In 1986 Bobby became a born-again Christian. To write
about the change in him would take me for ever, but I
thought he was a crackpot when he first told me and
obviously I found it hard to believe. The result is that we
are now true friends, closer than brothers. He is easier
to work with and if I have any problems he not only
listens but he also tries to help. That is some change, I
can tell you!

I see the future as very bright indeed and we can only
grow from strength to strength.

Now a little about myself. I also have made a commitment to God and have become a born-again Christian. It
is the biggest change in my life, and I have to tell you
it's FANTASTIC!

I am very proud to have put forward these few words
for this book. It will not be remarkable for its literary
style but for the simple truthfulness of a man who made
a commitment that changed his life. Anyone reading this
book, Christian or not, will find it fascinating, and it will
add weight to Christianity.

TOMMY CANNON

Acknowledgments

Here are some people I would like to acknowledge without whose help this book would not have come to publication.

James Catford   for allowing the opportunity to write.
Tommy Cannon   for his support and faith in me.
My children   for not interrupting me when I wanted them to.
Mavis Kershaw   for her valuable information about our childhood years.

But most of all I would like to thank Yvonne for her incessant nagging, for without it this book would never have been finished.

Thank you, all.

BOBBY BALL

1

'Our Bobby'

Life for me began on January 28th 1944 in the Boundary Park Hospital, Oldham. I was the youngest of three children born to Mr and Mrs B. Harper. My father had told my mother that she would have to keep having children until she gave him a boy. His first two children were girls, so when my mother gave birth to me my father was overjoyed, at last he had a son, a child that would grow up to be like him, a great sportsman. Oh, how his dreams would be shattered.

Life for my sisters and myself as children was very hard, just above the poverty line. I am still amazed at my mother's inner strength, at how she managed to feed us and keep us clothed. To this day I am still astonished that she managed it.

Home for us was a condemned house, high in the hills overlooking the cotton village of Shaw. Today it is more like a bustling little town than the village I knew as a boy. My father used to tell me that there were more cotton mills in Shaw than anywhere in the whole of Lancashire. They have all gone now, but when I was a boy the dark satanic mills with their huge chimneys climbing high into the sky gave Shaw a personality of its own. The house that we lived in had a character of its own too. The front and only door led directly into the kitchen, it had a flag floor and a stone sink that was about two inches deep; in the old days this was called a slop-stone. In one corner of the kitchen stood the stairs that led up to the bedroom and in the other corner was a whitewashed door that led to a cellar. The kitchen led into a living-room which had about eight mullioned windows overlooking the fields. We didn't have curtains, because the walls had deteriorated so much that it was impossible to attach anything to them. I remember my father once trying to put curtains up and the bricks and plaster started to fall down, so we never bothered. As my father said, 'It is better to have bricks and mortar than curtains.' We had an old unvarnished table in the centre of the room with newspapers on it instead of a table-cloth. And I remember my mother changing the newspaper every time we ate. She used to laugh and say, 'Well, at least we have something to read while we are eating.' But underneath her laughter I suspect she secretly longed for her own brand-new table-cloth with roses crocheted around the edges. Against the far wall stood a magnificent old cast-iron fireplace, with ovens at either side and a stand for putting a kettle on. Today that fireplace would be worth a fortune to an antique dealer, but in the early fifties everyone thought they were old-fashioned and wanted the new small-tiled fireplaces that had become fashionable. What a shame that sometimes what we think of as new is not as good as the old. But I loved that fireplace.

Late at night my sisters Mavis and Sylvia would sit in the ovens and I would sit on my mother's knee in front of a warm fire, and she would tell us stories of when she was a child.

Upstairs there was one bedroom and a landing at the top of the stairs that could just fit a double bed, so the two girls slept on the landing. And I, being the only boy, slept in the bedroom in a single bed at the far corner of the room.

At night, whenever it started to rain my mother had a ritual. She would get as many as ten pots and pans, and place them around the bedroom. I can see myself now watching her as she looked up at the ceiling and placed the pots and pans in the exact positions on the floor. Then as the rain started to come in, the different-sized raindrops would hit the different-sized pots and pans, creating a kind of nature's symphony. Many a time I would lie awake in the dead of night listening to the raindrops' music.

But the centre of my imagination was the cellar. It had about twelve stone steps leading down into the darkness. And in my mind there were about twenty different monsters hiding down there waiting to get me. I imagined them hiding in corners, just waiting for me and whispering to one another, 'Here comes Bobby, get him, get him.' I'm sure I met a few of them disguised as humans, as I got older. The cellar was definitely a hell-hole for me when I was a child.

It was my eldest sister Sylvia's job to light the fire before my mother and father got home from work. And we kept the coal down in the cellar. And who do you think had to get the coal? That's right, you've guessed it. Me! No matter how much I argued, I always ended up having to get it. Eventually I got the task of getting past the monsters down to a fine art. My biggest ally in getting the coal was my other sister, Mavis, a red-haired girl, who I'm sure could have fought any boy in Shaw and won. She was, and still is, one of my closest friends. She was always there when I needed her. And for that I shall be eternally grateful. Anyway, I digress. Back to the saga of getting the coal. My sister Sylvia would say, in her authoritative voice, 'Robert, go and get the coal.' (My family always called me Robert, never Bobby.) I would try looking at her with eyes that would melt an iceberg, but it would be to no avail. I knew I would have to get the coal. I would look at Mavis, who knew exactly what I was going to ask, before I had even asked her.

'Mavis,' I would ask, 'will you stand at the top of the steps of the cellar, while I get the coal?'

We had no electricity or hot water and certainly no such thing as a torch. So I used to light a piece of rolled-up newspaper, then we would stand at the top of the steps leading down into the cellar and peer into the darkness. After a second or so of building up my courage I used to set off at breakneck speed, throw the lighted paper on the floor, shovel up a shovelful of coal and run as fast as my little legs could carry me, back up the steps to safety. And all the time our faithful Mavis would be shouting, 'Robert! Robert!'

I felt good, because once more I had eluded the clutches of my imaginary monsters.

I know that some of you may be wondering where the bathroom was. Well, we didn't have one! We had to get washed in the slop-stone sink. And the toilet was outside across the common, and whenever we were taken short we had to run hell for leather across the common hoping we could make it in time. Our old toilet was a decrepit old thing with the door falling off its hinges. My mother used to cut up pieces of newspaper and hang them on a piece of string behind the door. Toilet paper was a luxury we couldn't afford. The toilet had a long wooden seat with a hole in it, and underneath there was a tin for our waste. Every week the council used to have to come and empty it. Great job, eh! Next door's toilet had a seat with two holes in it so that they could pass the time of day. I have always found that funny.

As I mentioned, we had no electricity or hot water, so bath nights were a special event. My mother used to boil kettles of water and fill an old tub which, when not being used for bathing us, stood in the middle of the stairs full of dirty clothes that needed washing. Bath night was usually twice a week. If my mother had given us clean water for each child, she would have been boiling kettles for weeks. So she would fill the tub once, and we would all have to use the same water. And guess who always got washed the last? Me! And guess who my mother always seemed to wash the longest? Me! I hated bath nights. The water seemed to be so hot that I felt it was going to take my skin off. And to this day I can't take a hot bath, the water must be tepid. My mother used to scrub us with a scrubbing-brush. I used to wriggle and writhe, trying to get away from the stiff bristles, but my mother always seemed to reach every nook and cranny of my body.

'Keep still,' she used to say. 'Cleanliness is next to godliness.'

I'll bet my mother still thinks that to be clean of body makes one closer to the Lord. What she doesn't realise is that one's soul has to be clean before one can get close to God. No amount of scrubbing with a scrubbing-brush was going to bring me closer to God.

After nearly scrubbing me down to my bones, my mother would then proceed to wash my hair. But not for us nice-smelling shampoos, oh no! We had to have good old-fashioned Derbac soap. Guaranteed to kill all head lice! Yes, you've read it right. Head lice. Just after the war it was quite common for children to get head lice, or nits as we used to call them. Why they acquired that name, I'll never know. Even when we went to school an inspector would come round checking the children's heads for lice. She was lovingly known as Nitty Norah the Nit Nurse.

After my mother had washed my hair in Derbac soap she would dry me off. And then I would have to kneel in front of her while she proceeded to go through my hair with something I can only describe as belonging in a torture museum, the dreaded Derbac comb. It was designed to catch any nits that were lingering about in your hair. It was a little steel comb with teeth so close together that none of the lice could escape. My mother used to pull the comb through my hair with such force that I felt that my head was going to come loose from my neck. There must have been a salesman somewhere in England, going around selling these things.

'Roll up, roll up, don't forget to buy your Derbac soap, guaranteed to kill all nits, and if you buy two, you get a free Derbac comb.'

I have never found anyone yet who will admit to selling them. Great days, eh!

As I sit here, attempting to write this book, many thoughts and images from the past keep passing through my mind. The old coconut matting we used to have, because my mother and father couldn't afford a proper carpet; my father always whistling and his clogs ringing on the flags; the long hot summers we used to have; my sisters playing out, in just their knickers, and me in nothing at all. (Don't start tutting, I was only a baby!) Everything seemed so innocent then. My mother chasing the rag and bone man down the road, trying to exchange an old rag for a piece of donkey-stone. A donkey-stone was a piece of crushed stone made into a block, and was used to clean the front door step and window-sills. I can still see my mother on her hands and knees scrubbing the front door step with her donkey-stone, and my father sitting on a stool talking to her.

Memories. Funny things, memories, I've got millions of them. And I wouldn't swop a single one, because for all the hardship I had a wonderful childhood, and a more loving family a child couldn't have asked for.

My eldest sister, Sylvia, was a little older than Mavis and me and had just discovered boys, so Mavis and I used to do everything together. Wherever I went Mavis was there. Whenever I played with my mates, Mavis was there. Mind you, I was glad of this because she used to protect me; and if anybody was picking on me our Mavis used to beat them up. (Thanks, Mave. You were a right little tomboy.)

Across the road from us lived the Waddingtons, Frank and Alice, and they had two children who became our best friends, Frank jun. and Denise. Old Frank Waddington was a farmer and used to deliver milk all around Shaw. Every Saturday morning I would rush out of the house just in time to see Old Frank going past in his milk float, with Dobbin, his old horse, pulling it.

'Come on, Bobby,' he would shout.

And I would run as fast as I could to catch up, and jump on to the back of the milk float, fighting to get my breath. Then Old Frank would let me take the reins. The old horse would slowly plod on, taking everything in its stride. But to me as a child that was the greatest horse in the world.

'Come on, Dobbin,' I would shout, and then start making a clicking sound with my mouth. Boy! It felt good.

When we reached a row of houses Dobbin would stop and Old Frank would jump off the back with his bottles of milk and start to deliver them. Then Dobbin would set off again and stop at the next row of houses, with me holding the reins. I felt I had so much power. Me! Such a little child, in charge of such a big animal. What I didn't realise until I was older was that I had no power over Dobbin at all. He had been going around the same streets for so many years that he automatically stopped and started on his own. And there was I, thinking that I was driving him. What a wally I was ... Old Frank must have had many a quiet laugh to himself.

I remember the Saturday morning our Mavis decided to join us; she ran with me and jumped on the back of the milk float. The first place we had to go to was down a bumpy lane called the Button Hole. As we set off our Mavis stood on the back of the milk float. For some reason that morning she thought she was a princess. There she was posing, lost in her imaginary world. Suddenly the cart hit a bump. Our Mavis fell off, landing in the

muddiest puddle in the lane. There she sat, mud all
over her, on her dress, in her lovely red hair; she was
covered from head to toe. Suddenly she had turned
into a real life Cinderella. Children can be cruel, and I
started to laugh at her as we carried on down the lane.
She started to cry. And then she ran home, never to be
a princess again. To this day she has never forgotten
that. She says that it wasn't falling off the cart that hurt
her. It was that her brother and friend left her sitting
there (sorry, Mave).

As far back as I could remember, my mother had
always been a cotton worker and my father had always
worked in the same factory. The factory produced asbestos. Looking back, my father has been very lucky not to
have caught some sort of illness through working in the
close proximity of asbestos the way that he did. He had
to travel quite a distance to work, so we got up at five
thirty. The bus left at six o'clock. So my mother used to
make up his sandwiches for his dinner, and then get us
ready for the nursery. My father's sandwiches were
always bread and dripping, he said he loved them. He
used to say they were good for you, he said the dripping
used to stick to his ribs and it helped to keep the cold
out. The people in Shaw used to say that my father was
better than an alarm clock, because they could hear him
coming by the sound of his clogs and his whistling.

After my mother had got my father off to work she
would start to get us dressed and herself ready for work.
And on the cold dark winter mornings our Mavis and I
would sit there shivering on the settee, waiting for our
mother to dress us. Our Sylvia would dress herself,
because she was already going to school and didn't need
my mother's help.

We were only allowed one comic between us. So on
Tuesday mornings we had the *Beano*. Tuesday mornings
were the highlight of the week. But of course with us
only having the one comic between three children there

were the inevitable arguments, with our Sylvia saying
she should have it because she was the eldest; and our
Mavis saying she should have it because she never got
to read it first. And then there was me, who never argued
but just looked at my mother, and giving her my best
'nobody loves me' look, could guarantee to get the comic,
nine times out of ten.

Once I had the comic I would start to read it. And my
sisters would sit on the edge of their seats, waiting for
me to finish. So I would read it slower, sometimes reading
the same page twice. Then my sisters would start moan-
ing to my mother.

'Mam, he's doing it on purpose,' our Mavis would cry.

And our Sylvia would look at me with all the venom
in the world, her eyes narrowed.

'I'm going to kill you if you don't hurry up!' she would
whisper.

I would look at my mother for support. And among all
the arguing she would just look at me patiently and say,
'Hurry up, Robert, I'm going to be late for work.'

Thinking back, my sisters were right. I was a horrible
little creep.

My mother worked at the Lilac mill. It was a huge
cotton mill with its own ballroom on the top floor. It was
a beautiful place. The ballroom had a huge polished
dance floor and a stage that held a full orchestra. And
all around the perimeter of the dance floor stood wicker
armchairs and tables. It was very luxurious. The Lilac
was one of the best mills to work at in Shaw. They seemed
to provide for their workers, which was a rarity fifty years
ago. The men and women used to start work at seven
thirty and finish at five thirty, with an hour for dinner.
And at dinner-time the men and women used to come
up to the canteen the mill owners had provided for
them, and have their dinner. They had a nurse on
duty and a welfare officer, Mrs Wolsenholme. I really
liked Mrs Wolsenholme, I think mainly because I was

her favourite. Every dinner-time she would put records on for the workers in the ballroom, and after they had eaten their dinner they would go into the ballroom and dance for half an hour; sometimes the workers would forgo their food and dance away the full hour that they had for dinner. Sometimes she would put concerts on for them. There they would be, dancing away, then back to the drudgery of the cotton rooms. One Saturday night in every month they would hold a dance and all the workers would turn up in their best clothes to dance the night away. I remember going to quite a few of them. It was great fun for a child, skidding round the ballroom floor, pretending to dance like the adults, and being able to get away from the watchful eyes of our parents for a few minutes.

Next door to the ballroom was the nursery, where young parents could bring their children to be looked after while they did a hard day's work. This was the place my mother used to take us every day. I remember the winters were very hard. We used to set off for the nursery about six thirty in the morning while it was still dark. We had to go down the Button Hole lane, through the fields and over a hill called the Haydings. The cold wind would blow through our thin clothes and my ears would turn blue. I hated those winter mornings. Sometimes my mother would pick me up and snuggle me into her, and it felt good, feeling the warmth of my mother. I would try to bury myself under her clothes, away from the cold wind. Picture the scene if you can. A woman in an old coat and head-scarf having to walk three or four miles carrying a small child, with two other children hanging on to her coat, battling against the cold winter wind. Every now and again she would put her tiny hand around one of the children hanging on to her coat, as if to give them reassurance. This was my mother. She stood only four foot ten, but she had an inner strength that made up for her lack of inches.

I remember a story that my mother used to tell us. I was only a baby at the time, and with us living on the moors we always got the snow first. That particular year, 1947 to be exact, was a very bad winter and we had no coal to keep us warm. So my mother told us to stay in bed while she went to get some coal. My mother's best friend was a woman named Elsie Henthorn, whose family was as poor as ours. Their husbands had gone to work, so together they decided they would walk three or four miles over the moors to an old coal pit to see if they could find any loose coal around the pit entrance. So off they set across the snowbound moors, dragging behind them two sledges to put their coal on. Finally they reached the coal pit entrance, and found some old pieces of coal lying around. They loaded up their sledges and set off home through the snow. When they got about a mile from our house, the string attached to my mother's sledge broke, and all her coal went tumbling down the hill, lost in the deep snow, never to be seen again. My mother said she just sat in the snow and broke her heart. I never knew whether she managed to bring any coal home or not, but it didn't matter, we survived. And funnily enough a few years ago I was walking through Shaw when I looked in a photographer's window. Unbelievably there was an old photograph from 1947 of my mother and Elsie Henthorn pushing an old pram up the hill through the snow. I immediately bought the photograph and gave it to my mother. And that photograph is on her wall today.

At the nursery I had already become a little star. I was about two or three at the time, and the radio had a programme on called *Workers' Playtime*. They used to visit different factories in different towns and meet the working people. Well, they finally got to Shaw, and where did they record the programme from? That's right, the Lilac mill! Mrs Wolsenholme must have told them about this little boy who couldn't stop telling nursery rhymes and singing. So they asked me if I would do something

for them. Would I? There was no stopping me. I was a
right little show-off. Anyway after a lot of persuasion
(about a second) I decided to recite a little poem my father
had taught me: 'I had a little pony'.

> I had a little pony,
> It was a dapple grey,
> I lent it to a lady
> Who rode it a mile away.
> She whipped it, and she lashed it,
> She rode it through the mire.
> I would not lend my pony again
> For all my heart's desire.

That's the poem I recited on the radio when I was only
two or three years old. I'll bet I was a right precocious
little brat.

Another time I was playing in the nursery when I
decided to be Superman. I climbed on to the top of the
gate and with the shout of 'SHAZZAM' (that is what
Superman used to shout), I dived off, heading for a pile
of cushions not far away. Yes, that's right. I wasn't Superman and I couldn't fly. Down like a lead balloon I went.
Crash! My head bounced off the floor like a basketball in
the hands of a Harlem Globe-trotter. Needless to say I
had a few bumps, but worst of all I had bitten my tongue
and it was hanging off. The nurse let my mother know
and then they rushed me to hospital. I didn't know what
was happening but apparently they sewed my tongue
back together. They told my mother that she had to take
me back the following week for them to see how it was
going on. My mother took me back, quite panic-stricken.

'Doctor,' she said, 'I think our Robert has swallowed
his stitches.'

The doctor looked at my mother as if she had gone
mad.

'Mrs Harper,' he said, with a smile on his face, 'your Robert hasn't swallowed his stitches.'

'But he has,' my mother insisted, 'I looked at his tongue last night and the stitches have disappeared.'

'I know,' the doctor said, 'we have used dissolving stitches.'

'Oh, I see,' said my mother, and took me home.

But to this day I'm convinced that my mother still thinks that I swallowed my stitches.

Every year Mrs Wolsenholme would put together a children's concert for the workers at dinner-time. It was always a very lavish affair with proper costumes that Mrs Wolsenholme had spent all year making. We wore make-up, and we had a band. Mrs Wolsenholme used to make us rehearse during the days prior to the concert, and as the day approached the atmosphere got quite intense. This particular year I had to sing a song called 'I'm the rich Maharaja from Matador'. So I had to wear these baggy trousers, pointed shoes and a turban. I also had to wear dark make-up, covering my face and body, to make me look as if I came from Morocco or somewhere. And our poor Mavis was a harem girl. She had to stand behind me through the whole song, fanning me the whole time with a huge cardboard fan. For about three days before the concert I kept telling our Mavis that she wasn't fanning me right.

'You're fanning me too fast,' I would say, or, 'You're fanning me too slow.'

This was getting on her nerves, and on the morning of the concert she finally snapped.

'You're not doing it right, Mave,' I said once again.

Suddenly I heard this almighty crash and felt something hit me on the head. It was the cardboard fan.

'I'm not doing any more,' said Mavis, and ran off crying.

Needless to say Mrs Wolsenholme calmed everything down and our Mavis went on stage that afternoon to become a huge success as a fan carrier. But Mavis, if you are reading this book, I still say you were fanning too fast.

One morning my mother took us to the nursery and there was a lot of commotion going on. We were being moved to a purpose-built nursery that had been built in the grounds of the Lilac mill. It was a beautiful place with all the facilities for looking after children. We had two nannies, Nanny Smith and Nanny Barlow. I loved Nanny Barlow, she was a lovely old lady with white hair and kind eyes. Nothing was too much trouble for her. She never seemed to lose her temper with the children, and she seemed to take a special interest in our Mavis and me, I think because we were the poorest. I continued to visit her till I was well into my teens. And I still called her Nanny Barlow until the day she died.

About 1948 it was decided that the Queen was to officially open the nursery, and all the workers were given a day's holiday. This was the biggest day that had ever happened in Shaw. All us children had to stand in a line when she arrived and wave these Union Jack flags that we had been given. To tell the truth I was more interested in keeping the flag than seeing this person who everybody was making a fuss about. The day arrived and we all stood in a line. Suddenly she came through the gate and we all shouted, 'Hurrah, hurrah,' with me shouting the loudest, wanting to be noticed. To me she seemed so important that she must be the most important nanny in the world. 'Hurrah,' I shouted even louder. She came along the line, every now and again stopping to talk to children. She's bound to stop and talk to me, I thought to myself, I've just been a maharaja in the nursery concert. But no, she walked straight past. I was bitterly disappointed. I met her later on in life and was tempted to tell her about it, but thought better of it.

There was one drawback at the nursery, the castor oil! We would stand in a line, with Nanny Barlow talking kindly to us and Nanny Smith at the end of the line dishing out the castor oil. She would hold out a large spoonful and I would screw up my face and gulp it down as quickly as I could, hoping that none of it would touch the inside of my mouth. Then came the nice bit, she would dip another spoon into a huge can of black malt treacle. It was so thick that you could have used it as damp-proofing on a flat roof. But I loved it. I used to let it linger in my mouth and savour the taste. Oh, I can taste it now.

So that's what it was like at the nursery when I was a child. And the friends that I made at the nursery I am still friends with today. There were Dennis and Glenys Henthorn, who were twins, and they didn't live far from us on the moors. Dennis was my closest friend all through my childhood. He was a very robust child with blond curly hair and a laughing face. We had many adventures together. I remember one adventure with particular clarity because I didn't suffer because of it till maybe thirty years later. Dennis and I decided to go and play in the fields, so our mothers warned us not to go near the Clough mill lodge. This was a pool of water that was used to cool down the steam system in the mills. And, because we had been told not to go near it, Dennis and I naturally decided to go. I always was a rebel, a stupid one, I agree, but nevertheless a rebel. When we reached the lodge we decided to play boats, so we got two twigs and proceeded to float them in the water. As luck would have it, my twig started to float away from the edge and, me being the stupid kid that I was, I leaned over to try and get it back. And plop! Before I knew where I was, I was in the water and going down. I remember I kept coming up gasping for air and seeing Dennis's face looking at me on the bank. Suddenly Dennis had hold of my hair and was pulling me up. I finally got out looking and feeling like a drowned rat. Now Dennis and I were in a bit of a dilemma because we couldn't tell our mothers what had happened as they'd warned us to stay away. So we decided to see if we could dry my clothes. I took them off and hung them on a tree and stood there naked as the day I was born. I was freezing. After about an hour of watching my clothes not getting any drier we decided to tell our mothers a story that would get us out of trouble. I put my wet clothes back on and Dennis and I got down to plotting. We decided to tell them that we had gone for a walk and met some boys who had thrown me into a river and Dennis had saved my life. Yes! We decided it was a good story. So we set off for home with this lie firmly planted in our brains. The nearer we got home the bigger the lie became. When we reached home and walked in the front door my mother threw her hands in the air.

'Whatever has happened?' she shrieked.

Dennis proceeded to tell her our story and I just stood there in my wet clothes trying to look as sorrowful as ever. My mother looked at Dennis and then at me. I felt very worried for a moment that she had seen through our lies. Suddenly she gave Dennis a hug.

'You've been a very good boy, Dennis,' she said. 'You have saved our Robert's life.'

And with that she opened her purse and gave Dennis a shilling. We had got away with it. Dennis said thank you and left and my mother pampered me for the rest of the day. Dennis and I spent the shilling the next day on toffees. Thirty years later when I was about thirty-six years of age I told my mother the truth. Much to my surprise she suddenly hit me across the head and said that the shilling she had given Dennis was the only money she had at the time, and that I deserved the slap she had just given me for telling lies. It just shows that lies find you out no matter how long it takes.

There are other faces I remember. One was Billy Lupton, the nursery bully. Everyone was frightened of him, even our Mave. He was bigger than any of us and was continually battering us. But as he got older he changed and is now one of the nicest men you could wish to meet. Not long ago I went fishing with Billy and we had some great laughs, remembering the old times.

And then there was Dennis Cockeroft, a big lad who had a wonderful soprano voice. He and I would always be competing to see who was the best singer.

It was at the nursery that I also met my first love, Ann Sheriff, a little girl with black hair and nice clothes. I thought she was wonderful, and used to look forward to going to nursery to see her. She was to me what dreams were made on. I even used to give her my gobstopper toffees, but it was to no avail, she didn't like me. If I had known then what I know now, I wouldn't have given her my gobstoppers. You see, no girl was worth a gobstopper in those days, least of all one that didn't like me.

Then there was our Jack Harper, my cousin. Jack didn't live far from us, so we had our own little gang that played together all the time. There were Frank Waddington jun. and his sister Denise, Dennis and Glenys Henthorn, our Jack and me. Oh, and I mustn't forget our Mavis.

I remember quite vividly the winter of 1949. It was one of the worst winters Britain had ever seen. Up on the moors where we lived the snow had drifted to twenty foot deep. It was freezing, so my mother had to put more coats on the beds. We didn't have blankets so she used to buy old coats from jumble sales and put them on the beds for warmth. But the cold didn't bother us kids, we were having a great time. My father had made us a sledge and it was the best one I had ever seen. So with my new sledge and the snow so high, I felt I was living on a different planet. The gang and I would take our sledges to the top of a road called Roses Brew and sledge all the way down. When we reached the bottom we wouldn't stop, because then we hit a flat piece and carried on down another brew called the Newt Brew. It was a run of about a mile. When we reached the bottom we would have to walk all the way back to the top, but with me being the youngest, our Mavis would have to drag the sledge. On the way back to the top of Roses Brew, snow would collect on the bottom of our clogs and we called these cloggybobs. The snow on our clogs would make us two or three inches taller. And it was great fun trying to walk, because the snow on our clogs made us slip more. But woe betide any of us who didn't knock it off before we got home. Our mothers would play heck with us for walking all that snow into the house. It was quite sad for us to see the snow we had collected left outside the door, like an old friend that you no longer wanted.

It was only when I started writing this book that our Mavis told me that when she saw other children with shoes she felt envious because she thought they were rich. It's funny, but I was the closest person to our Mavis all her life and only found that out a couple of weeks ago.

The weekends were a special time for me. My mother and father weren't working so we did everything together as a family. Friday evenings my father would come home from work, have his tea, and then if we'd had any coal delivered we would all carry it in buckets down into the cellar. I didn't feel afraid of the monsters then, because they seemed to disappear when my dad was there. And when we weren't doing that, we would do some other job. Then my father would get washed. I can see him now, standing in front of the slop-stone washing himself in freezing water before changing into his clothes. When he had done that, he would put on his flat cap and clogs, give us all a kiss and go off to the pub. We would be able to hear him whistling as he walked off into the distance. The fire would be burning in the grate and my mother would finish all her chores and sit down wearily in an old armchair. We had no television then, so my mother would say, 'Let's have a concert.' And my sisters and I would entertain her by putting on little shows. About ten thirty we would hear my father coming down the road, whistling. We would jump into the ovens at the side of

the fireplace, and wait for him to come through the door.
In he would come and hang his flat cap on a nail behind
the door. It was very exciting for us because we knew
that he would start to tell us stories about his family,
and that meant we would be able to stay up a lot longer.

Every time my father went out without my mother he
would bring her home a bottle of Mackeson's stout. She
loved it. He would pour the stout into a glass and then
put the poker in the fire until it was glowing red hot, then
he would put the red hot poker into the glass of stout. I
would watch the black stout, fascinated as it fizzled and
frothed, trying to fight the heat of the poker. Then my
mother would drink it (without the poker in it, I hasten
to add). My father used to say it was the best drink anyone could take, because when the poker went into the
drink small pieces of iron would disintegrate into the
stout, making it a drink that was good for the blood. I
never fully understood that when I was a boy, but as
I grew older I could see what my father meant. My
mother was anaemic, you see, so my father was giving
her the equivalent of today's iron tablets that are used
for people with weak blood. My father had many remedies
like that.

After my mother had drunk her iron stout, my father
would sit me on his knee and tell us about when he was
a boy. The stories he used to tell us were fascinating.
His grandmother and the generations before her were
Romanies, travelling people. They worked on the fairgrounds, and travelled from place to place in their caravans. The fairgrounds in those days were much more
exciting than the fairgrounds of today, because it was a
special event when they came to town. There was much
more entertainment then because the fairgrounds had
side-shows, with bearded ladies, fakirs and all sorts of
weird and wonderful things.

My great-grandmother worked in one of the side-shows
as a snake charmer, and apparently was a great draw.

My father used to tell us one story about her, that one
day she brought a new snake, a huge beast of a boa con-
strictor. She had hardly worked with the snake when one
night she decided to put it into the act. She proceeded to
wind the snake around her. The audience must have been
amazed in those days to see a woman with this huge
snake wrapped around her. Anyway something must
have frightened the snake, because it started to constrict
its muscles and suffocate my great-grandmother. The rig-
gers, who used to put up the tents, saw what was happening and ran as fast as they could to help. One of them
pulled out a knife and slit the snake in two. As a boy
that story was always guaranteed to get my imaginative
juices flowing. I never knew what happened to my great-
grandmother after that but I always remember her as
the woman with the snake.

Those evenings sitting round the fire listening to our
parents telling us stories were unforgettable. We may
have been a poor family, but if love was money then we
were millionaires.

But Saturday night was the best night of the week for
me. It was club night. My mother and father would get
us ready and take us down to the Shaw Labour Club.
The club was situated in the centre of Shaw, and my
father being a Labour supporter thought of it as his club.
It had a concert room, where the parents could sit and
have a drink while watching the artiste who came to the
club every weekend. It also had a smaller room for the
children to play in. We were not allowed in the concert
room because they served alcohol, but we weren't particularly bothered, we had a great time on our own, playing
games and running up and down the stairs. Occasionally
they would break the rules and ask my father if I would
sing for them. My father would come and collect me from
the children's room and take me into the big concert
room. I felt very special. There I was, this little boy, on
this big stage among all these adults. I loved it. The

microphone was too tall for me, so I had to stand on a stool. It was very precarious. But it didn't matter, I still stormed them (I can't help being so modest). One night the pianist, Eric Barlow, started to play the introduction to the song I was going to sing. But when it came to my turn to sing I found I couldn't find the pitch of the song. Eric stopped playing and looked at me.

'What's the problem, Bobby?' he asked.

I just looked at him with a vacant stare.

'It must be in the wrong key,' he said, and started to play in another key. Suddenly I stopped him.

'No! No! Mr Barlow,' I said, 'that's not right.'

He stopped playing and just looked at me. Now he had a vacant look on his face.

'This is the key,' I said, getting down from my stool, and I hit one of the notes on the piano.

Like an automaton, Eric started to play. Unknown to him, all the notes on the piano looked alike to me, so I had just hit one, and luckily it was the right key. He just kept looking at me in disbelief. He thought I must have been a child genius. And to this day there is an old man walking round Shaw thinking that Bobby Ball was a wonder child.

Our Mavis and I used to sing together at home, so she eventually joined me on stage and we became good enough to be asked to sing every Saturday night.

On the way home from the club my father and I used to have races. He always let me win, but I always thought that I had won on merit. One night my father and I were racing and he fell. He pretended not to be hurt but I could tell by the look on his face that he was in pain. I had no idea at the time that it was the start of the arthritis that would bring this great sportsman down to a crippled wreck.

My mother and father started to take us to more clubs and the people there had heard about our Mavis and me so they started to ask us to get up and sing. We were getting quite famous in Shaw. One night when I was about five years of age we went to the High Crompton Conservative Club, which was about a mile out of Shaw. About half way through the night the committee asked my father if he would let me get up and sing. My father agreed and I got on to the stage, confident as usual, and proceeded to belt out a couple of songs. In the club that night there was a stranger, everybody could tell he was a stranger because he wore a trilby hat and everybody in Shaw wore flat caps, and besides that, he was a cockney. When I had finished singing he came over to our table and asked my father if he would mind stepping outside. My father thought the fellow wanted to fight, so he put on his macho voice and said, 'No problem,' and followed him out. When they got outside the man asked my father if he would mind sitting in his car as he wanted to talk to him. My father must have been impressed because there were very few cars in Shaw in those days and anyone who owned one was very wealthy. They sat in the car and the man said that he would like to manage me. This was all new to my father, so he asked him what he meant. The man said he would like to take me to London, because he had a song he would like me to record, and he would put me in stage school, because he thought I had potential, and would like to groom me to be a star. And he also said that he would give my father £500. My father was astounded, because in those days £500 was equivalent to £5000 today. My father told the man that no amount of money could buy his son, and that his son was staying where he belonged, with his mother and sisters. The man said he understood and gave my father £5. He told my father that the £5 was for me to have singing lessons.*

Needless to say I never had the singing lessons,

* I've sometimes wondered how my career would have turned out if my dad had accepted the offer and put me into a London stage school.

because the very next day my mother took the three of us down to the Co-op clothing store and bought us all new clothes. It was the first time we had had new clothes and they felt and smelled wonderful. I had new wellingtons, which were brown and yellow with a sheriff's star on either side. I also got a new raincoat, but that wasn't as great as the wellingtons. Our Mavis was over the moon because she finally got her first pair of shoes. And our Sylvia sulked because she wanted a blue raincoat instead of a grey one. Walking back home that day we all felt very posh, very posh indeed. There was I, jumping in every puddle I could find and our Mavis walking almost on tip-toe so as not to damage her new shoes, and our Sylvia still sulking, saying that young ladies didn't wear grey. That is a memory that will never leave me. When my father came home we all paraded in front of him showing off our new clothes. He then asked our Mavis for her new shoes and put cardboard in them. He said it would save the sole. Even to this day I've never understood the logic of that.

One day Denise Waddington came across the common to our house very excited. They had got a telly, she told us. To us they seemed to have the world, they had electricity and we only had gaslight. I thought Denise was the luckiest girl in the world. Anyway they invited us across that night to watch it. I remember sitting between old Frank Waddington's legs and watching a programme called *The Quatermass Experiment*. It was a science fiction play about a man who had come back from a mission to Mars and picked up a deadly disease. One day in the laboratory he accidentally touched a cactus and slowly his whole body turned into a killing cactus. It frightened me to death. Later that night, when it was time to go home, we had to cross the dark common and we ran as fast as we could, thinking that the killer cactus was behind us. For years after I couldn't pass a tree without thinking that maybe it would come to life any second.

We had many happy years up on the moors. Summertime would find us going for long walks and my father used to make us take old milk bottles with us and if we saw a stream, and the grass at the side of it had turned brown, he would make us fill the bottles. He said this was natural iron water, and was good for the stomach. I think he learned many of his remedies from his Romany ancestors. I remember once that my mother got a sort of a growth on the top of her thumb, and before long it was covering her whole thumb. She went down to the doctor's in the village, and he gave her some cream. She applied the cream for about a week but it wasn't doing any good. By this time my mother had stopped cooking because by now her whole thumb had become infected and she was frightened of contaminating the food. So my father told us children to go into the fields and collect as many dandelion flowers as we could. So we all went out into the fields and collected as many as we could. We came back with thousands of them (maybe I do go over the top a little, but after all I am in show business), and we gave them to my father who was sitting with my mother in the kitchen. We watched as he proceeded to split the stems and rub the juice from the inside of the stalks on to my mother's thumb. And within a couple of days the growth had started to go, and within a week it had disappeared altogether.

As a child I accepted this as normal but when I got older I realised that my father knew more about natural medicines than I gave him credit for. And I'm sure that in the world around us there are natural cures to fight many diseases.

The year now was 1949 and I had reached the grand old age of five, time for me to go to primary school. Like my two sisters, my mother sent me to the Shaw Wesleyan School. What she didn't know was that all my mates, such as Dennis Henthorn and our Jack, had been sent to the East Crompton School. I remember my first day at

school, our Mavis holding my hand taking me there. Our
Sylvia had already gone up to the Crompton House
Senior School. Our Mavis walked me into the playground
and stood with me until it was time to go to her class.
The time came for her to go and I was left with a load of
first-day children. Standing there I felt so alone, as if I
was heading into the unknown. Finally a teacher gathered us all together and herded us into a classroom. I sat
there at this desk wondering what had happened to my
world, and in particular what had happened to our Mavis.
I knew deep inside that this wasn't the place for me. The
kids at the school seemed different from the kids at East
Crompton School. The kids at my school seemed very
rich. After all, they had indoor toilets and electricity and
they had school uniforms. My mother had to get ours on
tick.

After school our Mavis and I would have to go to the
nursery and wait for my mother to finish work. And on
the way to the nursery we would stop at the river Beal
and fish for sticklebacks, with worms. But when I caught
one I couldn't take the fish off the worm so I just used to
let it dangle in the water. You know, thinking about it
now, I must have been a right stupid kid.

Eventually, with our Mavis being a couple of years
older than me, she left our school and went up to the
senior school. This left me really alone. But by now I had
got used to feeling not as good as the others, and besides,
I could fight them all. So our Mavis's leaving was not
that bad.

I remember one Thursday afternoon there was a lot of
excitement among the children at school. Friday was the
day that the *Topper* comic came out, and this week there
was a free gift with every copy bought. The free gift was
a toy called a Banger. It was two pieces of cardboard with
a piece of brown paper stuck between them. And when
you whizzed it through the air, it made a banging sound.
Friday morning came and I begged my mother for 3d to

buy the comic (in today's money that is equivalent to less than 1p). Anyway my mother gave in to my pleadings and gave me the 3d, which I doubt she could afford. As soon as I had the money I ran all the way down to Mr Parkinson's paper shop, which was conveniently at the side of the school.

'Could I have the *Topper*, please, Mr Parkinson?' I asked, eager to get my hands on my Banger.

'I'm sorry, Bobby,' he replied, 'we have sold out.'

My little heart sank. My disappointment was so huge that I thought I was going to burst into tears. Little did I know that disappointments would become part of my life.

'I'll have the *Beano* then,' I said, trying not to cry.

When I got into the school yard all the other kids had their Bangers.

'Harper! Where's your Banger?' the other kids kept asking, but I told them I didn't want the *Topper*, that I really liked the *Beano* instead. Inside I was as sick as a parrot!

Another event during my infant days that I vividly remember was when I was literally tarred and feathered. It happened when school was over and I was on my way to the nursery to wait for my mother. She had just gone into debt to buy me some new clothes for school and that particular day was the first day I was wearing them. It was the middle of summer and it was really hot. So I took my time (dawdling, my mother used to call it) getting to the nursery. Suddenly I came across a huge mound of tarmac at the side of the road, a child's delight if ever I saw one. I decided to see if I could run up it in one go. So off I ran, getting to the top in one go. What I didn't realise was that with it being so hot, the centre of the tarmac had melted. So when I reached the top, slop! I sank into the middle. I don't know how I managed to get out but I did. I was covered from head to foot in tar. It was all over my clothes, my head, my hair, everywhere.

I started to cry. If ever I needed the love of my mother it was now. I tried to run but couldn't, so I had to be content with walking like someone with two broken legs. By this time I had ceased crying and gone into the state of bawling. Everyone was looking at me as I made my way to the cotton mill where my mother worked. I knew that when I reached my mother she would put everything right. I finally reached the mill and went inside the big room that my mother worked in. The noise of the machinery was deafening and I felt lost among it all. My mother was nowhere to be seen. People began to stop what they were doing and look at me. Mind you, I must have looked a sight. I had suddenly turned black and was walking as if I had done something nasty in my trousers. I stood there for a while looking for my mother and didn't realise that all the cotton that was flying around the room was starting to settle on me. Suddenly I saw my mother looking at me with her mouth open at the far side of the room. This only made me bawl louder. At last I could see my sanctuary. I started to make my way to Mother, but the more I moved the more the cotton was sticking to me. When I eventually reached her I was truly tarred and cottoned. My mother just stood looking at me not believing her eyes. And I just kept looking back at her, wondering when she was going to make everything all right. Suddenly she gave me such a clip round my ear that I thought I wouldn't hear for a week. And this only made me bawl even more. By now I was sure that my bawling was louder than the machinery. Anyway she gave me a shouting at for ruining my new clothes that she hadn't even paid for yet and took me home. I don't remember much about it after that. Only that for the next few years whenever I saw a tarmac mound I gave it a wide berth.

With me now going to school, my mother allowed me to go with our Mavis to the 3d matinee. This was the Saturday afternoon performance at the local cinema, the

Princess, or the Prinnie as we used to call it. It cost 3d to get in. I used to wait eagerly all week for Saturdays. And when Saturday came our Mavis and I would run all the way down to the cinema and wait outside with the other kids. The doors would open and we would all dash in like mad marauders. There was no parental guidance at the 3d matinee, so you can imagine what it was like, five hundred kids screaming and flicking pieces of paper at the screen. It was total bedlam. But we all calmed down when the picture started.

They always ran a short film first and the one that was always shown was *Flash Gordon*. It had everything for children. It had a villain, Emperor Ming. And a goodie, Count Zarcoff of the bird people. He would walk around with two huge wings strapped to his back. But Flash would be the hero. It was a sci-fi serial and every week Flash would be left in a dangerous situation. Like, for instance, the spaceship with Flash in it would blow up and a deep American voice would say, 'Is Flash dead!!! Killed by a bomb planted on the spaceship by his arch-enemy Emperor Ming. Find out next week.' All the kids would sit there open-mouthed, wondering if they would ever see Flash again. But sure enough next week we would see Flash jump out of the spaceship just before it blew up. Marvellous stuff.

Then the main film came on, usually a cowboy one with great names like Hopalong Cassidy or Lash Larue. And we would all cheer or boo as the goodies and baddies appeared on screen. One could always tell the goodies from the baddies by the colour of their hats, the goodies always wore white hats and the baddies wore black ones. When the film was over all the kids would dash out of the cinema reliving what they had just seen. I was no exception. Off up to the moors I would run, making the sound of horses' hoofs with my mouth and pretending to be Black Bart, scourge of the West. And our Mavis would be running behind me, sulking, because I'd say she was

Sitting Bull and she would moan, saying that she didn't want to be an Indian. But nine times out of ten that's what she ended up being. And if you don't mind my saying so, Mavis, you were a very good Indian.

The year now was 1954, and I was ten years old, when my life suddenly changed. A man arrived from the council and told my parents that we could have a council house. Oh, the excitement that night in our house was overwhelming. They even had a choice. They could have a house on a local estate or a house that was one of a few at the end of a long street called George Street. They decided to take the house on George Street because, as my father said, 'It was built with *proper* bricks.' I never understood what he meant by that statement.

My parents informed the council that they would take the house on George Street, so the man from the council came back and told them that everything was okay and we could move into the new house in a week's time. I don't remember that week. But I remember the day of the move. My father had hired a wagon from Cuss the coalman to take all our meagre belongings down to the house. He filled it up with beds, the sideboard and whatever else we had. My mother had an old pram and anything that couldn't fit on the wagon we had to push down to the house in the pram. I remember my mother, Sylvia, Mavis and myself pushing this old pram full of things down George Street. It was only about a quarter of a mile long but to me it was the longest street in the world. It had no houses on it, just fields either side, with a huge oak tree in the middle. I loved that old oak tree, I don't know why, but it just looked so tall and majestic standing there. Later on in life when I had got married and moved away they pulled the tree down and built an estate where it once stood. I still drive past today and wonder how easily man can change beauty into ugliness. Gone are the fields and my beloved oak tree and in its place a housing estate. That's progress, I suppose!

Anyway when we reached our new house it was like a palace to me. Now I had what the other kids took for granted. We had a garden back and front and three bedrooms. And how's this for being posh, we had a front door and a back door, we also had an outside loo that we could actually flush. But the best thing was we had electricity and hot water. I felt we had moved up in the world. I think it was all too much for my mother because as soon as we got into the house I started switching the lights on and off because they fascinated me. My mother gave me a slap and told me to stop doing it, 'Because,' she said, 'the Germans would think we were signalling.' The war had been over nine years. But the stupidest thing was that I believed her.

We had now become respectable, for the want of a better word. Oh, and now that we had electricity my father bought us a television! I know that may not mean much to you, but to us it was one of the biggest things that had happened in our lives up to then. They used to stop broadcasting at ten thirty but we used to stay up and watch the dot disappear. We thought it was fantastic. Funny how we just take it for granted today. I suppose God feels like that sometimes.

For me at the age of ten I had other things on my mind. I was about to go up to the big school and enter a whole new world. There I would discover two things that would change my life. But more about them in the next chapter.

2

Brylcreem and brothel-creepers

The year 1955 was a big one for me. It was the year that
I started at the big school, Crompton House. Our Sylvia
by this time was already married, so there was only our
Mavis left at the school to see me through my first day.
The first day at Crompton House School was nerve-
racking because of a rumour that first-year starters had
to go through some sort of initiation ceremony.

Crompton House looked like an old mansion that had
been turned into a school. It was a very regal building
with mullioned windows and Gothic architecture, and
inside it had long corridors and staircases that seemed
to reach to the sky. It was the type of building that
wouldn't have looked out of place in one of Emily Brontë's
books. To an eleven-year-old it painted a very forbidding
picture.

The day arrived for me to go up to the school and for
me it was as if a whole new adventure had started in my
life. My mother had given me my dinner money before
she left for work, with the instructions that I was to
behave myself and listen to our Mavis. I didn't listen to
her as I was now eleven years old and thought I was old
enough to take care of myself. At eight fifteen our Mavis
and I set off to catch the bus that would take us up to

the school. Over the years I grew quite fond of that bus, because I had so much fun on it. It was a single-decker bus and it didn't have a number but the letter F. We called it the little F. Anyway we boarded the bus and before I knew where I was, we were getting off right outside the school. I just stood there looking at this huge school that was like stepping into the unknown. All sorts of things were going through my head. I was wondering what the future held and feeling all the time that I didn't really belong. That same feeling has been with me all my life until a point when something happened to make things very different indeed.

Our Mavis and I had to separate, she to the girls' playground and I to the boys'. I slowly started walking towards these huge gates that led to the boys' playground, my mind going wild with fear, because now I was about to be initiated. Let me explain about the initiation, which was called 'slabbing'. At the side of the playground was an old stone slab where the older boys used to grab the new boys on their first day, put them on the slab of stone and smack their bottoms with their plimsolls. As I walked through the gates I could see that some other young boys had been slabbed because they were crying, but I was determined not to cry. But for once I was alone and didn't have our Mavis to fight my battles. Suddenly it was my turn to be slabbed. The fourth-formers, Brian Greenwood, Joe Hagan and Bobby Henthorn (Dennis's elder brother) and the others, turned and looked at me. I was the smallest of all the children in the school, apart from Bobby Jelly (his real name) who was even smaller than me. For some reason they must have taken pity on me because they left me alone and I was never slabbed. (That didn't stop me slabbing other kids when I got to the fourth year.)

After my first day life at the big school wasn't too bad. Our Mavis was always there to rely on, and Dennis and Glenys Henthorn started the same day as me, so at least

I was surrounded by friends. I seemed to make friends quite easily so before long I had quite a few. There was John Bodkin, whom I still see nearly every week, he's the local butcher now in Shaw. Then there was Dennis Howarth. I saw him again after about twenty years and he looked just the same as he did when he was seventeen. Lucky devil! There are a lot of other friends I could mention but if I did it would leave less space to talk about me.

I remember one particular day when I was in my first year at the school. We had just left at four o'clock and were on our way home. Down the back of the school was a dirt lane and this was a short cut. When I was half way down the lane I started to have a fight with another boy and just as I was beginning to win a voice boomed out from the top of the lane.

'Harper!'

We stopped fighting and looked up. There stood Mr Stanhope, a young teacher all the girls were in love with.

'Harper! See me in the morning at the first lesson,' he shouted.

That night I didn't sleep. Inside I was panicking. It was the first time I had been in trouble at the school. I kept wondering what was going to happen.

Morning came and our Mavis and I caught the little F bus up to the school. I never told our Mavis, so she didn't know what torture I was going through. We arrived and were soon in assembly for morning prayers. I kept sneaking looks across at Mr Stanhope but he didn't look at me once. When prayers were over we all made our way to our different classes. My first class was religious study. With who else but Mr Stanhope! I sat there all the time wondering when he was going to call me out in front of the class and cane me, but he didn't, he just kept looking at me, and for some strange reason didn't say anything. At the end of the lesson he dismissed us all and we all started to leave. I felt so relieved. I had got away with

it. Just then he shouted, 'Harper!' My heart went into
my mouth. Now was the time. I slowly turned and looked
at him. He looked back at me and winked.

'Forget about it, Harper,' he said, 'but don't let me catch
you fighting again.'

'No, sir!' I replied and was out of that classroom as fast
as Linford Christie.

I have never felt so much relief in my life. But I couldn't
understand why he had let me off. From then on he
gained my respect and became one of my favourite
teachers. I think it was because he didn't treat us like
children but like friends. I also realised when I got older
that he didn't punish me because he knew I would put
myself through enough punishment worrying. He was a
good teacher. And if you read this book, Mr Stanhope, I
want to thank you for your compassion.

During all this time I had continued singing, but by
now our Mavis had joined me and we had become a double
act, 'Bobby and Mavis'. To be honest, we had become
quite successful for a twelve- and fourteen-year-old boy
and girl. My parents had obtained a licence from the
education board that allowed our Mavis and me time off
school to entertain, so we used to travel all over the place
at weekends as a professional act. At weekends we would
go over to Yorkshire to work in the clubs. Our Mavis and
I, with my mother chaperoning us, would set off and catch
the train to Sheffield, then we would go to the club and
perform. After we had finished our performance we would
get paid and that would pay for our digs for the night;
when we got paid from another club the following night,
that would pay for our train fare home with a little bit
of spending money left. I remember one weekend we were
supposed to perform at the same club all weekend, with a
Sunday dinner-time show thrown in, which meant extra
money. As usual we set off and caught the train to Sheffield. When we arrived at the club it was quite busy so
we went on stage and paralysed them. When we had

finished my mother asked the concert secretary for our
money, but he told her that we wouldn't be getting paid
until we had finished the weekend. I can still see my poor
mother's face. Panic and defeat swept across it at the
same time. We had no money to get back home and we
hadn't enough money for digs. We sat in the dressing-
room and all was quiet for a moment or two and then my
mother stood our Mavis and me in front of her and told
us the situation. To me as a child it seemed a great adventure but to my mother it must have been a problem that
seemed to be insurmountable. There she was, penniless,
with two children, somewhere in the backwoods of Sheffield looking at the prospect of spending the night on the
street. It was ironic really, there were our Mavis and I
on stage with the audience going wild and my poor
mother sat backstage wondering what we were going to
do. She told the concert secretary of our predicament but
he told her he couldn't help because it was against the
club's policy (nice man, eh). Everything must have
seemed hopeless to my mother. At the end of the night
we had to stand at the entrance of the club and tell people
we had no money and ask them if they could put us up
for the night. It must have been degrading for my mother.
She must have felt like a beggar. Anyway God must have
been smiling on us because a lovely couple said they could
take my mother and our Mavis in but they didn't have
any room for me. Thankfully God smiled once again when
the organist from the club said he would take me in. Our
problem was solved and we said our goodbyes. I knew
that my mother was worried because she had never been
separated from her children before, but to me it was a
great adventure. We arranged to meet the following day
at the club and waved to each other as my mother and
our Mavis went off with their hosts and I went off with
mine. We reached the organist's house and his wife made
such a fuss of me that I felt like a king. She made me
cocoa and gave me cakes, it was terrific. Even now as I

am writing this I smile at the memory. Anyway Sunday morning arrived too quickly and we set off for the club. When we arrived my mother was already waiting. She welcomed me with open arms and then she started to attack me with a barrage of questions.

Was I all right?

Had I been a good boy?

Had I given any cheek?

Before I had time to answer the organist put his arm round my shoulder and told my mother she should be very proud of me, because I had been a very good boy (I'm sorry, reader, I'm beginning to feel sick myself).

We finished the lunchtime show and then we had to find some way to spend the afternoon until it was time for the evening show. So we went down to Sheffield bus station and watched the buses going to their different destinations (riveting, eh). Evening came and we went back to the club for the evening performance. It went down very well and the concert secretary paid my mother and for the first time that weekend we felt independent. All through my life I strove to be independent of people, to ask no man for anything, to be my own man. It wasn't until later that I realised being dependent on someone could be a good thing.

By the time I had reached thirteen our career had really started to take off. A cousin of mine by the name of Wally Harper was a professional comedian and he had taken us under his wing and started to manage us. We were doing warm-ups for BBC radio, which meant we got to meet all the great stars of the day like Ronnie Hilton, Lita Rosa, Jimmy Clithero and many more. A television producer by the name of Billy Scott Comber had also taken us under his wing and was teaching us a comedy routine based around the song 'I'm for ever blowing bubbles', which meant our Mavis singing it straight with me doing the comedy. We had to go down to the BBC every weekend and rehearse the routine and Mr Comber told us that when we were ready he would put us on a popular television show called *Comedy Bandbox*. It looked as though I had a very successful career ahead of me. But it was not meant to be because something came along to change my life. All that year I did the warm-ups, practised the comedy routine and did the clubs as well as going to school as much as I could.

One year we got a booking at the Majestic Hotel in the Isle of Man for a whole fortnight. Since everything was paid for, the whole family decided to make it a holiday. The Majestic Hotel was a magnificent place overlooking the harbour, and we were the resident act there. We lived like kings for a whole fortnight. They had a talent competition running and the prize was a recording contract and an audition for a television show. We were not allowed to enter because we were the resident act and were classed as professionals, and the talent show was for amateurs only. One day a good-looking young man arrived at the hotel on an old Lambretta scooter with a beautiful girl on the back. He asked the manager if he could enter the talent competition, but was told he was too late; the competition was that night. The young man looked very sad as he walked out of the hotel and my father must have felt sorry for him, because he stopped him and promised to have a word with the manager. The young man seemed pleased and waited while my father tried to persuade the manager. After a while my father came back and told the young man that he was in the competition. The young man was delighted and went on to win the competition. His name was Gerry Dorsey who later became Englebert Humperdinck. Many years later Englebert did one of our TV shows and I reminded him of the time in the Isle of Man. He remembered it and thanked me for it.

In 1958 my life changed. I had reached fourteen when suddenly I discovered girls. But more importantly I discovered rock 'n' roll. Instantly Little Richard, Chuck

Berry and Jerry Lee Lewis became my heroes. All these stars made a big impression on me. James Dean and Elvis seemed mean and moody and that's what I wanted to be. I began to think that anybody in show business was a sissy. To me Elvis and James Dean were real, I couldn't imagine them in show business, so it was time for me to get mean and moody. The first thing I had to do was to tell our Mavis that I didn't want to do the act any more.

I told her that I couldn't be bothered any more and she accepted it without any qualms. Little did I realise that she may have discovered boys and rock 'n' roll herself.

So the first thing I did was to get a jar of Brylcreem and plaster it on my head. The idea was to get a rock 'n' roll hairstyle. To do this one had to comb one's hair into a style called the elephant's trunk. This consisted of combing it up at the sides and down over the forehead. At the back we used to comb it so that it made a parting down the centre of the back of the head. This was called a DA. The Brylcreem would make your hair greasy so that when you combed it, it stayed where you wanted it to.

Now this worked fine on people with straight hair but with me having curly hair it only made it curlier. So you can imagine how I must have looked. I looked like a Rastafarian that had just seen Freddy Kruger. Nevertheless I felt good. The next thing to come were my drainpipe trousers. These were trousers that were as tight as you could get them. And I have to tell you I don't have the greatest legs in the world. Then came my brothel-creeper shoes, my bootlace tie, and – the last thing of all – no rock 'n' roller would be seen dead without his shirt collar turned up. This made one look really mean and moody.

But at school we had to dress as schoolchildren should dress.

There was one girl at school I was really attracted to. She was gorgeous-looking with long blonde hair. The only fault was that she came from the posh part of town and as I came from the opposite end she seemed out of my reach. Every day I used to see her running down the corridors and my heart used to melt. Of course I didn't tell anyone except Dennis Henthorn, I didn't want them to think I wasn't mean and moody. So secretly I used to look at this girl and know that she could never be mine. One day Dennis came over to me in class and said that he was taking a girl to the pictures that night and asked me if I would go with them. I told him no, because I said I didn't want to be the gooseberry. He told me not to worry as he had got me a date, and the girl he had got me a date with was the girl of my dreams. I couldn't believe my ears. He told me he had asked her if she would go out with me and she had said yes! My heart started pumping and I had never felt as excited in my life. That evening I spent hours getting ready, getting my elephant's trunk to look its best, making sure my drainpipes were pressed. Eventually I was ready. I wore a new casual jacket that I had just bought, it was brilliant, because when I turned the collar up it came half way up my face. The only problem was it was made of plastic, so I could smell plastic all the time. But it didn't matter, it was truly a rock 'n' roll jacket. (Thinking about it now, I must have looked a right little wally. I was only about four foot eight.)

I met them all at the Princess Cinema and when I saw her I couldn't speak, she looked beautiful. I just nodded my head in her direction and then looked the other way. That must have made me look really mean and moody. We all went into the cinema and sat in the back row, Dennis with his girl and me with mine. The lights went down and the movie started. I hadn't even plucked up enough courage to talk to this girl yet. My mind was ticking over at a hundred miles an hour. Should I hold her hand? Should I ask her if she wants an ice cream? No! I thought, I'm going to go for the big one, I'm going

to put my arm round her. After about ten minutes of
courage building I slowly sneaked my arm around the
back of the seats and on to her shoulders. To my amazement she didn't resist. There I was, me, sitting with my
arms around my dream. My confidence had grown by this
time to an all-time high, so I decided I would go for the
really big one, the KISS! I waited until the time was
right, then I slowly turned my head towards her. She
looked back at me and I knew that the time was right.
We slowly leaned towards one another, our lips pucker-
ing, she with her eyes closed and me with mine wide
open, not wanting to miss a moment. Then at the crucial
moment, we kissed, or I thought we did. But no! Her eyes
shot open. My collar had come between us. Her lips were
kissing one side of the collar and mine the other. I can
still see her eyes looking at me over the collar. I'm sure
she must have felt nauseated by the smell of plastic. Anyway my confidence was shattered. In her eyes I was no
longer the boy who was mean and moody, but the boy
who smelled of plastic. This was too much for me, with
all my credibility lost I ran out of the cinema. Even my
elephant's trunk was fading. I had just blown my chances
with my dream girl and I hadn't even spoken to her.

The next day Dennis asked what had happened. I
couldn't tell him the truth, so I told him I didn't like her,
because I fancied someone else instead. I realise now that
instead of putting a front on I should have told the girl
in the first place that I really liked her. Who knows what
may have happened? But it's funny how we go through
life pretending to be what we are not.

I think 1959 must have been one of my favourite years,
because I reached fifteen years of age and was in my last
year at school. The careers officer had been round and
given me up as hopeless, but then again what did he
know, he didn't know rock 'n' roll. I had become a bit of
a rebel at school (my mother didn't know, she would have
killed me). I was in my last year so like every teenager

down through the ages I didn't think about the future,
only the present.

One Monday morning we had to assemble in Mr Davis's
class. Mr Davis was my least favourite teacher. He was
a big man who could frighten people just by looking at
them. Anyway this particular morning he was scowling
more than ever. When all the class were seated he told
them that on the previous Friday they had all misbehaved and that they had to do half an hour's detention
after school. Well, I thought this was very unfair on me
as I hadn't been at school that day, so I decided to tell
him. I put my arm up to get his attention as children do,
but he seemed to ignore me.

'Excuse me, sir!' I shouted.

He looked at me with venom in his eyes. I'm sure he
hated me more than anyone in the class.

'What is it, Harper?' he replied.

'Well, sir,' I began, 'I wasn't at school last Friday,
so I don't think it's right that I should have to do detention.'

He just looked at me. 'You will do detention with all
the rest of them, Harper,' he said.

Now all my life I have believed in people being fair
and doing the right thing, and I thought that Mr Davis
was being unfair so I decided to tell him.

'But, sir,' I shouted from the back of the class, 'I wasn't
there that day, so I won't be stopping for detention.'

The class went silent, at last somebody had stood up
to this bullying teacher. Mr Davis's head shot up from
the book that he was marking and looked at me as if he
was going to kill me. But I knew I wasn't going to back
down, because I knew I was right.

'Harper!' he shouted. 'Come here.'

I started my long walk from the back of the class.
Everybody was looking at me and I was beginning to
wonder whether I should have kept my big mouth shut
and done detention instead. But no! I knew I was right.

When I reached Mr Davis's desk he was already glaring at me.

'You, Harper,' he said, 'will do as you are told and you will stay in for detention with the others after class.'

'No I won't, sir!' I replied defiantly.

'Yes you will!' Mr Davis bellowed.

'Oh, ———,' I said, swearing at him in my best James Dean voice.

I could see the rage start to rise from his toes as he rose up to his full six-foot height.

'What did you say?' he screamed.

'Nothing, sir,' I replied innocently. I then turned to the class, 'Did I?'

And with one voice they replied, 'No, sir.'

This was too much for Mr Davis, already it looked as if his face was going to burst with blood pressure. He reached out and tried to grab me. I was too quick for him and dodged, but I knew I had gone too far and it was time for a quick exit. I bolted out of the classroom, thinking I was safe, but when I turned round there was Mr Davis in hot pursuit. Suddenly there was this giant of a man chasing me through the corridors of the school. I ran as I had never run before, but he was catching up, so I headed up the stairs to the headmaster's office. When I reached there I didn't even knock, but just barged in with Mr Davis a hair's breadth away.

Mr Hargreaves must have wondered what on earth was happening. It must have seemed that a hurricane had entered his office. There we stood, me, this small boy, and this giant of a man, both gasping for breath. It took Mr Hargreaves a couple of minutes to find his voice, then he finally said, 'What on earth is going on?'

Mr Davis was the first to reply. He told Mr Hargreaves that I had refused to do detention and that I had sworn at him in front of the whole class. Mr Hargreaves was always a fair man and that day was no exception. He asked me if what Mr Davis had said was true and what

had I got to say for myself. I put on my best innocent
voice and told him the truth, that I hadn't been at school
the day the class misbehaved so I didn't think it was
reasonable that I should be punished. Mr Hargreaves just
nodded his head and said he understood. Then he asked
about Mr Davis's accusation that I had sworn at him.
Now this is where I have to confess I lied. I looked at Mr
Hargreaves and told him that Mr Davis was lying and
he could ask the class if he wanted to. Mr Davis nearly
had a heart attack from anger, he started ranting and
raving that I was a disruptive force in the class and so
on and so on. Mr Hargreaves finally calmed him down
and told me that I had got away with it this time, saying
that he believed that I shouldn't be punished for something that I hadn't done, but on the other hand he
believed Mr Davis that I had sworn at him. So he said
that we must let the whole matter drop but I wasn't to
start bragging to the other children, or I would be in
trouble. He dismissed me and told me to go back to my
class while Mr Davis and himself had a talk.

I left the headmaster's study feeling that I had won a
major battle. When I got back to the classroom all the
other children were waiting to see what had happened.
I just smiled very broadly and put my thumb up, a cheer
went around the classroom. Of course I ignored what Mr
Hargreaves had warned me about and told them all the
details. I became a hero for a day. As for Mr Davis he
never looked at me again and left me alone for the
remainder of my time at school.

At weekends a few friends and myself had started to
travel up to Oldham, which was about six miles from
Shaw. This was big time because Oldham was a town
and we came from a village. We used to go to a place
called the Green, which was only a common but it had a
fairground. The main ride was the Waltzer, and the teddy
boys used to gather there and listen to the rock 'n' roll
music. We were no exception. We would stand around

the Waltzer, pretending to be tough by puffing on one of the five Woodbines we had just bought around the corner. It was the Green that led me to my first wife.

One weekend I spotted a girl I fancied very much and decided to have a go at pulling her (that's teddy boy talk), so I eventually got talking to her and found out that her name was Helen Lavity. We seemed to get on very well and she even told me where she lived. We arranged to meet the following weekend on a date. I thought this was going to be the start of a big romance. The following weekend came but she never showed. I was devastated, so I decided to go and look for her (I can be terribly clingy when I want to be). I took my friend Dennis Howarth with me (you never went on your own at that age) and we went around the streets of Oldham looking for her. When we reached the street where she lived I saw a red-haired girl who was very pretty. She was just on her way to the shops so I decided to ask if she knew where Helen Lavity lived. She told me she knew her and asked me why I wanted to know. I told her that I had a date with her and then unwillingly confessed that she had let me down. She told me she could understand that as Helen Lavity was already going out with somebody else. I wouldn't go as far as to say that I was heartbroken, but I will admit that my heart felt a little pang of depression. Anyway we chatted for a while, with Dennis holding the candle, and then we said our farewells.

The following weekend a few mates and I went up to the Green again, and a gang of girls was there, among them Helen Lavity and the red-haired girl. It was funny but I found myself looking at the red-haired girl. Eventually the gang of girls split up leaving the red-haired girl and a friend on their own. I put on my best Elvis face and walked over to her and started talking. I found that I felt very much at ease with her, it was as if I had known her all my life. She told me her name was Joan Lynn and that she didn't have a boyfriend. This was the start of a long courtship which eventually ended with her becoming my wife.

Our romance was a very hit and miss affair at the beginning, with me seeing her only at weekends. Funnily enough I had started to see another girl at the same time, one who lived near me in the next village, so I used to see her in the week-nights after school and Joan at the weekends. (Don't be too hard on me, I was only fifteen at the time.) The other girl's name was Margaret Fielding, and she was very tall. The truth is I had to stand on two bricks to kiss her. No wonder my arms are longer than they should be, it was carrying those bricks around all the time.

I remember one time that it was sports day at school. A few of my mates and I were no good at sports and I knew it was going to be a very boring day, so I hatched a plan to escape from the boredom. When the whole school arrived at the sports field, all those that were competing would go on to the field and those that were no good at sports would sit on the perimeter and cheer on the competitors. Now I couldn't see the sense in sitting there cheering for something that I wasn't vaguely interested in. So I told my mates that when we got down to the sports field we should all sit at the back. When the sports and all the cheering started, in the commotion we could sneak out under the fence one by one, then we could spend the day with Margaret Fielding and her friends. My mates readily agreed, so the plan was on.

Sports day arrived and we all went down to the sports field, my mates and I making sure we sat at the back so as not to be seen. The plan went like clockwork, the cheering started, we all sneaked out and before long we were all on our bikes pedalling towards an afternoon of fun. We spent the day hanging around the bus shed in the centre of the village flirting with the girls, without a thought for the others at the sports day. We thought we were the clever ones. Little did we realise.

The next morning came and before I knew where I was, I was in assembly listening to Mr Hargreaves telling all the other children who had competed in the games how clever they were. Not as clever as us, I thought to myself, we had taken the afternoon off. When he had finished his speech he went very serious for a moment, then he said, 'Five boys were seen running away from the sports field.'

I suddenly started to sweat, I didn't think we had been seen.

'And now,' he continued, 'would they please walk to the front of the assembly hall, and take their punishment like the men they think they are.'

Sneakily I looked around the room at the others to see what we were going to do. They were obviously just as frightened because they were sneaking looks back at me. I decided to take the whole issue into my own hands. I figured that if I started to walk forward the others would follow. I pushed my way through the other children and started to walk down the centre aisle towards Mr Hargreaves. A deathly quiet had come over the room. I began to get a strange feeling that I was alone. I quickly turned round and looked behind me. My feelings were correct, not one of my mates was behind me. I felt totally naked. Even the girls in the assembly were looking at me as if I was some kind of gremlin. But it was too late to turn back now. I carried on walking towards Mr Hargreaves, with every step getting heavier with fear. The assembly hall had a stage that Mr Hargreaves used to stand on so that he could address the whole school, and this morning was no exception, so that meant I had to go up on to the stage. I'm sure by this time I was walking the way I did when I fell in the tar. I slowly walked up the steps that led to the stage and stood in front of him. He looked down at me but didn't say anything for a few moments. This only made things worse.

'What have you got to say for yourself?' he asked finally.

'Nothing, sir,' I replied, lowering my eyes.

'Who were the other boys that were with you?' he asked, tapping his cane against his leg.

I looked at the others standing in the assembly, and they looked back at me, their eyes pleading with me not to tell. I didn't answer. This only made Mr Hargreaves angrier.

'Harper!' he bellowed. 'I am waiting for an answer.'

Again I refused to answer.

He asked me once again, 'Who were the boys that were with you?'

'I was on my own, sir,' I lied, not daring to look at him. This only infuriated him more.

'Well, Harper,' he said, 'seeing that you were on your own, you won't mind taking the punishment for the other boys that were with you then, will you?'

'No, sir,' I replied, dreading what was coming next.

'But seeing that you were honest, Harper,' he continued, 'I am not going to punish you.'

A flood of relief ran through my body. I had got away with it. But my hopes came crashing to the ground with what Mr Hargreaves said next.

'But as there were another four boys with you,' he said, 'you will take their punishment instead.'

All the time this was going on I expected my mates to suddenly come running forward to own up. But perhaps I was expecting too much. I could hear Mr Hargreaves's voice droning on somewhere in the distance, but I was lost in my own thoughts.

'Harper!' His voice brought me back to reality.

'Did you hear what I had to say?' he said.

'No, sir!' I replied.

'I asked you what are four threes.'

'Twelve, sir,' I answered, now realising that I was going to get twelve whacks of the cane.

'Very good, Harper,' he said. 'Now step forward.'

I stepped forward and held my hands out. Whack! The cane landed twelve times, six on each hand. I felt as if I had stuck my hands into a bramble bush. I bit my tongue, there was no way that I was going to show that it was hurting me.

When he had finished my hands felt like they were on fire. I felt like crying but I held my tears back, and stood there defiantly. He told me to go back to my place and not to let it happen again. I walked back to my place in the assembly, occasionally looking at my mates, but they couldn't look at me. When we got into the playground they said they were sorry and how brave I was to take twelve lashings of the cane. I forgave them, because I knew that if I hadn't been so stupid as to walk forward I would have done the same as them.

Meanwhile my love life took a twist. Margaret Fielding found out that I was going out with a girl from Oldham and finished with me, so Joan and I started courting quite seriously. My schooldays were nearly over and I would soon be waving goodbye to Crompton House without many regrets. What I wanted to do with the rest of my life I had little idea. If you had told me then that I would end up as a famous comedian one day I would probably have thought *you* were being funny.

3

Clock-on Tommy

By the end of 1959 I had left school. As I had no qualifi-
cations, I ended up working in the cotton mill. It was quite
a funny experience leaving school and going out into the
real world. My mother used to pack up my sandwiches
and I would set off to work with her (she worked at the
same cotton mill). The first day they put me down in the
cellar where all the bales of cotton were kept, and my
job was just to follow the cellar foreman around doing
any jobs he told me to do. About this time I became
friendly with a boy who was to become my best friend
for some time. He is still one of my closest friends. We
have been through many experiences in life together, and
I know that he is a man I could rely on if ever I needed
him. His name is Trevor Kershaw, and if you read this
book, Trevor, I just want to thank you for everything that
you have done.

Anyway I'm digressing again. I stayed in that job for
as long as sanity would allow, then I moved to another
cotton mill. For the next twelve months it was just going
from cotton mill to cotton mill. It didn't matter, all I lived
for was my social life. I used to meet Joan on Fridays,
Saturdays and Sundays and then it was usually with my

mates; and during the week we all used to mess about in Shaw.

I remember one Thursday that my mates and I decided to go to Oldham to see a film. While in the cinema I met a girl and we got talking. I asked her if she would meet me in Shaw the following night. She agreed, so I said I would meet her at seven o'clock at a place called Wren's Nest in Shaw. Friday came and I realised I had got two things wrong, first I had to see Joan that night and secondly I had no money to get to Oldham where Joan was. I asked my mother if she could lend me some money but she said she didn't have any, so I worked out another plan, one that was sure to get me my bus fare to see Joan.

Seven o'clock arrived and my mates and I were waiting for the bus to arrive at Wren's Nest. As we were waiting I started to worry in case the girl wouldn't turn up, because if she didn't my plan would fail. But my worries were unfounded because when the bus arrived she was on it. I greeted her and we started talking while my mates hung around. After about ten minutes I asked her if she would excuse me for a minute while I had a talk with my mates. I gathered them together and asked if any of them wanted to buy her off me for a shilling (the price of my bus fare to Oldham and back). A lad called Graham Lees, whom we had nicknamed Leo, said he would, and he gave me the shilling. I told the girl I had to go somewhere and that Leo would look after her, but not to worry because I would be back later. She was obviously put out by this, but I didn't give her time to argue because I jumped on a bus and was away. (I know what you're thinking, but I couldn't help it, it was just circumstances that made me a white slave trader at fifteen.) Anyway after I had seen Joan I caught the bus home to Shaw. On the journey back my conscience began to bother me. I realised that what I had done was wrong, so when I reached Wren's Nest I went looking for them. I had a vague idea that they would be in a wooded area called

Dunwood Park, and sure enough I was right, because when I got there I could hear them all shouting. Now I didn't know whether it was a case of gang rape or just the lads messing about, but I wasn't about to take that chance. I knew I had to get the girl away from them but I didn't know how. Then I had another idea.

'Police,' I shouted at the top of my voice.

And all the lads scattered in different directions leaving the girl on her own. I love it when a plan comes together. The girl was so glad to see me that she forgot about me selling her for a shilling and allowed me to walk her home. I never saw the girl again but for some reason I've never forgotten her.

My courtship with Joan grew more serious as months went by and I started to see her on a regular basis. There was only one problem, my friend Trevor didn't have a girlfriend, so more often than not he used to hold the candle (play the gooseberry) for Joan and me. One day Trev and I were talking and he told me he had always fancied our Mavis. The next day I told our Mavis that Trevor fancied her and asked her if she would go out with him. She agreed, but told me she was only doing it for me as she didn't fancy *him*. (Strange how things turn out. Trevor is now my brother-in-law and they have been married for almost thirty years.) Anyway we started going out as a foursome and became quite inseparable. But it nearly ended one year when Trev and I decided to go on holiday with his brother and his friend. We had booked a holiday at the Golden Sands Holiday Camp in Rhyl. We were all staying in an old run-down caravan; but it didn't really matter about the state of the caravan, I was still young and this was the first time I had been away without my parents. So to me it was really an adventure. Our Mavis and Joan saw us off at the bus station and Trev and I acted as if we didn't want to go, but inside we were very excited. We arrived at the caravan and settled in. There were four of us in it so you can imagine the state it was soon in. But it didn't matter because we were on holiday without the girlfriends. Yippee!

About a week into the holiday I entered the talent competition they were running at the camp and won it. The prize was two book-ends, which by the way my mother has kept for more than thirty years. Anyway, in the competition was a young girl called Moira whom I found very attractive. True to the old saying 'When the cat's away, the mice will play' I started to flirt with her. She told me she was staying with her parents in a caravan not far from ours. I was a little disappointed about this, because I was hoping she would be on her own like me. But she said if I went late at night she would leave her bedroom window open and if I was quiet I could sneak in, because her parents would be asleep. Now this was very exciting, because not only was I going to get a girl but I was about to become James Bond for a night. The following morning came and Trev woke up feeling ill. As the day went on he became decidedly worse, so off to the doctor's we went. The doctor told him he had caught a virus and gave him some tablets. I tried to look after Trev with as much compassion as I could, but I found it difficult as I kept thinking about sneaking into somebody's caravan that night. Ten o'clock arrived that night and Trev was already asleep, because the tablets the doctor had prescribed were making him feel drowsy. This was turning out to be a great holiday! In those days you never went anywhere without your mates, even on a date. And tonight Trevor was going whether he liked it or not, even if I had to carry him there. So all night I kept giving him cups of coffee trying to keep him awake. About one thirty in the morning I looked at him and he was fast asleep, so I woke him up and told him it was time to go. He hadn't got a clue what was happening, but out of loyalty he followed me, not that he was much company, by this time he was like a zombie. I slowly made my way through the maze of caravans with Trevor following me like one of the living dead, and eventually we reached Moira's caravan. The pitch-black darkness all around us made everything seem quite eerie. I knew what a thief must feel like.

Gingerly I knocked on Moira's bedroom window, and waited for her to open up. She didn't, so I knocked again, still no window opened for me. I realised that she had fallen asleep. So once again I knocked, only louder this time. Suddenly all the lights in the surrounding caravans lit up, including Moira's. I was out of there like a seagull with its bottom on fire. The last I saw of Trev he was half asleep wandering towards the swimming pool.

The holiday was soon over and we arrived home. I told Joan I had missed her so much and that next year we would go on holiday together. About a fortnight after we got back Moira came looking for me. Luckily I was in Oldham with Joan. But apparently Trevor had seen Moira in Shaw looking for me and for some reason he took her to our house. My mother asked her who she was and invited her to wait for me, but our Mavis told her in no uncertain terms that I was courting and that was the end of that. Moira left and when I got home I got the third degree, my mother asking how did I come to meet her, our Mavis calling me a two-timer and Trevor just standing in a corner laughing. Everything was smoothed over, and Joan never found out. If she had done, perhaps my life would have turned out totally different.

My teenage years found me going from job to job, until eventually I started working in the building trade for a chap named John Pogson. He was a wonderful Christian man who took me under his wing and treated me like a son. He has been dead a long time, but to me he was one of the nicest men I have ever met. I stayed working for John for about twelve months then the wanderlust got the better of me again and I moved on. I found a job in an engineering works as a labourer and the money was good so I decided to stay a while.

Meanwhile my social life had taken another turn. With Joan, Mavis, Trevor and I becoming such close friends we had decided to form an act. Trevor played the drums while the girls and I did the singing. We had some great times going around the clubs. We called ourselves the Black and Tans, because I was the only one with black hair while the other three had flaming red hair. We thought it was a great name, until the day we worked at an Irish club. I can tell you we didn't go down too well. And to tell the truth we weren't half bad.

My father by this time had become practically stone deaf and though it was a handicap for him, for us it was brilliant. In the lounge we had our record player, an old Dansette, and an old upright piano. The piano was situated just behind my father's chair. I can still remember the nights we used to have our favourite Elvis records ('Jailhouse rock', 'A big hunk of love') on at full blast, and there we would bop the night away, while my father read his paper, without a clue about what was happening. But that was all to end when my father said that he had decided to get a deaf-aid. It didn't mean much to our Mavis and me because it wasn't going to change our lives. How wrong we were. He went for some tests and they finally agreed to let him have one. He came home with this thing protruding from his ear, looking very proud. We began asking him questions in whispers and to our amazement he answered them. It must have been wonderful for him to hear again. He said he could hear the birds once again. It's amazing how we take things for granted, when they can be taken away at any time. As time went on we got used to his deaf-aid, although it was a pity we couldn't have our records on full blast any more. One day when I was in the kitchen I asked my mother in the barest of whispers if she could lend me £1. Suddenly my father's voice boomed out from the lounge.

'No, you can't!' he shouted. 'You have had your spending money.'

I knew then that no longer could I get away with anything because my father could hear even a whisper from the kitchen.

By the time I had reached eighteen, our Mavis was already married to Trevor, so that left only me at home. Next door to us lived an old lady called Mrs Tarkenter and her niece Emmy. She was a lovely old lady who kept herself to herself, but as she got older she started to lose her mind and go a little crazy. I would always arrive home about eleven o'clock after seeing Joan, and Mrs Tarkenter would start waiting for me. She would stand at her bedroom window in a long white night-dress, with her long black hair flowing over her shoulders, beckoning to me. It terrified me. (When I was young I had watched the play *Jane Eyre* on TV and the mad woman in the attic frightened me to death. To this day I am still frightened by deranged women.) Anyway the more crazy Mrs Tarkenter became, the bolder she got. One night I arrived home at my usual time and saw Mrs Tarkenter waiting for me at her window. I ran as fast as I could down the garden path to our front door. The worst part was getting my key out and letting myself in. My imagination would run wild. What if she came now? What if she came running up the garden path, screaming at me with a knife in her hand? These thoughts and many more ran through my brain as I fumbled with my key. I got in and banged the front door behind me. Then I breathed a sigh of relief, at last I was safe. My mother and father were always in bed when I arrived home so I made myself a cup of tea, and tried to put her out of my mind. I turned on the TV and settled down to watch my favourite programme, *The Twilight Zone*. Just as I was getting into the programme I heard a tapping on the window. It was Mrs Tarkenter. This was the first time she had ever done anything like this. My skin began to crawl. I was so terrified I couldn't move. I could hear her moving around outside looking for a way to get in. I knew I had to get upstairs, but the only problem was that the stairs that led to the bedrooms faced the front door. I decided to make a dash for it and get my dad. He would know how to handle the situation. As I opened the door that led to the stairs, I could hear Mrs Tarkenter at the front door. I pressed my back against the wall and tried to sneak past the front door. Just as I was going past the door she lifted the letterbox and started to call my name.

'Robert, let me in,' she whispered.

I turned around and looked at the door. There she was peering at me through the letterbox. She was looking right at me and whispering. I shot up the stairs like a bat out of hell. I woke my father telling him that Mrs Tarkenter was trying to get into the house. He must have thought that I had gone mad myself. He got dressed and went downstairs. I can see him now telling her off as if she was a little schoolgirl, with my mother and me watching from the top of the stairs. She went from bad to worse, wandering around the gardens at night, attacking her niece Emmy, who left her when she couldn't take any more. She died eventually and the sad thing was that she wasn't found for two days. I still regret that I hadn't helped her more, because I can see now that she was only calling out for help. Maybe some day through God's grace we will meet and if we do I will take her in my arms and ask her to forgive me.

In 1964 I had reached twenty and Joan and I decided to get married. Our Mavis had just had her first child, Beverley, so we could no longer carry on with the act. During all this time I had been going to night school to learn how to become a welder. Joan and I saved up enough money to put down a deposit on a little terraced house in Oldham. We got married and moved into our house. She was very patient with me because I decided to decorate it myself. I started with the bathroom, and at that time I was in what I call my psychedelic period. I painted the walls in very vivid colours of blues, reds and greens and then I painted over the top of them in clear varnish. I often wonder what the people who took over our house after us thought.

But 1964 was a turning point for another reason. It was the year I met a man who was to become my closest friend for the rest of my life, my mentor, the brother I never had. Tommy. I had gone to the factory that day as usual, and as usual I was late. But it didn't matter because my mate Terry Brierly used to clock me in. So I would turn up late and sneak behind the machines and nobody was any the wiser. This day I arrived and Tommy stood by the door waiting for somebody to show him what to do (it was his first day). I noticed how lonely he looked so I said, 'All right, cock!' which for anybody that doesn't know is an Oldham greeting. He just looked at me and nodded. Anyway I sneaked behind the machines and got on with my job, not thinking any more about it.

Friday nights were always special because that was the night all the boys used to go out, it was a kind of a ritual in northern towns around that time, and it was always called the lads' night out. We used to all meet up in the town and go around the pubs, then when the pubs had shut we would always end up at the Candlelight Club. It was a bit of a dive really but I have to be very careful about what I write because the club is still going and the owner is a friend of mine. Friday nights in Oldham in those days were fantastic. It had one main street, Yorkshire Street, going from the top of the town to the bottom, a distance of about half a mile. There must have been about fifteen to twenty pubs on that stretch and every one had a group playing there – many of them later became famous including the Beatles. This was our Friday night out, the lads and me hitting every pub on the way down Yorkshire Street. It was a pretty lively place to be on Fridays. The only problem was that none of us had a car, so we were pretty limited to where we could go.

I noticed that Tommy had a car so I asked him if he would like to go out with us all on Fridays. Luckily he said he would, so now we had a car to go out in. We had really gone up in the world. I will always remember that little car of Tommy's, it was a Mini, but not just an ordinary Mini, that wouldn't have suited Tommy. It had alloy wheels, two radio aerials, and chequered racing tape down the side. It was a brilliant-looking car. He was always a poser! Friday nights were never the same after Tommy agreed to go out with us, now we had the freedom to go wherever we wanted. I had started singing again so began to do the clubs at weekends. I wasn't bad but I wasn't brilliant either. I was quite happy then, thinking that life was good. I was totally unaware of how things were going to change for me.

In 1965 Joan was expecting our first child. It's strange but when you are young you accept that your wife is pregnant without particularly seeing the beauty in it all; you just get on with life. It is only when you get older that you see the wonder of it all. Joan was always frightened of hospitals, so she decided to have our baby at home. It was an experience of a lifetime, I can tell you. When the time arrived for her to have the child Joan told me I should phone the doctor as she was experiencing labour pains. I knew something was happening as I was beginning to feel sick and sweaty and was suffering a terrible backache. Anyway I rushed up to the phone box at the end of the street and phoned the doctor. He told me not to panic as he would send a midwife round immediately. The midwife came round and examined Joan. She told her that she wouldn't be ready for a long time yet and that she would be back nearer the time. Little did we know that Joan would be in labour for twenty-eight hours. I was in a terrible state. I sat downstairs with Joan's dad and Joan was upstairs with her mother. Eventually the midwife returned and with her help Joan delivered our child. Downstairs I heard the baby cry and then the midwife shouted to say I could go upstairs and look at the child. When I entered the bedroom the first thing I looked at was Joan. She looked worn out, but that was understandable after twenty-eight hours of labour. Then I saw our child. Joan had given me a son, and he was the most beautiful baby I had ever seen. He had a huge curl on the top of his head and the biggest, bluest eyes you ever saw. The in-laws took a look at him and then left. Now there was only Joan, the midwife and myself. The midwife told me that on the top of the cooker there was a kidney-shaped dish with a rubber tube in it, and she asked me to sterilise it.

'No problem,' I told her, 'now that I'm a father I'm very responsible.'

How wrong that statement turned out to be. Downstairs I went to sterilise the tube. After a while the midwife turned to Joan and said that she could smell burning. Joan said she could too. So the midwife came downstairs to check that everything was all right. There was the new responsible father fast asleep on the settee with the rubber tube burning in the dish. Being irresponsible came naturally to me for the next twenty years. The next morning Joan's mother came down to find me sitting on the edge of the bed, in my donkey jacket, with my guitar.

'What the hell do you think you are doing?' my mother-in-law demanded to know.

I told her I was serenading my son. (He wasn't even a day old yet and already I wanted him to know how talented his dad was.) Next to arrive was the midwife to see if everything was all right. She asked me if Joan had had her breakfast yet. Oh no, I said, I forgot. So I dashed up to the corner shop and bought a jam roll cake, a chocolate roll cake and a slice of angel cake. I took them home and sliced them all into pieces. I set them all out on two dinner plates and proceeded to take them upstairs. I felt very proud because I felt I was helping. I can still see the midwife's and my mother-in-law's faces when I entered the room. Their mouths dropped open, and they just stared at my assortment of cakes. Joan's face never changed because she was already used to my eccentric ways.

'Are we having a party?' the midwife eventually asked.

'No,' I replied, 'it's Joan's breakfast.'

They both looked at me as if I had gone crazy. What they didn't understand was that when I saw Joan looking worn out after having the baby, my stupid brain told me that she needed sugar for energy, hence the cakes. Well as you can guess the cakes didn't get eaten and my mother-in-law made Joan a nice cooked breakfast. I can't remember if she made me one, most probably not.

That year I was getting more gigs than usual, I was out nearly every weekend. Show business was starting to take over my life. Even at work it was all I could think about. It would eventually be the downfall of my marriage. I still went out with Tommy and the boys on Fridays and I occasionally went out in the week too. I was spending less and less time at home.

When I used to do a gig at a weekend, more often than not Tommy would show up with his wife and over a period we got to be really good friends. After a while Joan and I would visit Tommy and his wife at home and vice versa. Up to this point Tommy was not in the business, but I could tell that he was very keen. Meanwhile at work I got friendly with a lovely man called Stan Moores, who worked on one of the saw machines. In his spare time Stan played the organ round the clubs. He was a wonderful jazz pianist so I asked him if he would write some music for me. He agreed and invited me up to his house to rehearse. When I arrived there I was surprised to see that his wife was a girl I used to go to the Lilac nursery with. Isn't it a small world?

One day Stan told me he had been offered a resident

gig at a small working men's club not far from where I
lived. He said it was a good gig because it was every
Friday, Saturday and Sunday. But he said there was only
one problem and that was that he needed a drummer.
Now this sounded very good to me as I was getting tired
of going from club to club wondering if I would get any
more gigs or not. So I told him that I was available. He
asked me if I could drum, and I told him yes (I learned
to drum when I was in the Black and Tans, I used to
practise on Trevor's drums). I didn't tell him that I had
never played for acts before, but with my ego that was a
minor problem. He told me I could have the gig and that
I could start the following Friday. The only problem was
that I didn't have a drum-kit but Stan said not to worry
as there was a kit at the club which I could use. The
following Friday came and I arrived at the club ready to
start my career as a drummer. Luckily that night the act
that was on was a double act that did all Roy Orbison
numbers and I found that quite easy to do. I also used to
sing while playing the drums, between acts, and my big
number was 'Whiter Shade of Pale' by Procol Harum. The
members of the club hadn't seen anyone do this before so
I became quite a success there. I thought I could settle
there but it was not to be.

Every Friday Tommy and the boys would come into
the club to see me, then they would leave about ten thirty
and go up to the Candlelight Club, leaving me to finish
the gig. This was all right for the first few Fridays, then
I began to feel I was missing out on all the fun. I can
still see them now as they all got up at ten thirty, gave
me a wave and left, leaving me on the drums backing
some old lady singing 'I want to be Bobby's girl', which
got more and more awful as the song went on. I stuck
this for about two months and then I told Stan I was
leaving. He was a good man and he understood. So there
I was back on the road doing the clubs and every Friday
up at the Candlelight.

One day Tommy invited Joan and me up to his house for tea. I accepted the invitation, so our Robert (we didn't name him after me but after my father) was put into his carrycot and off we went. We had tea and then sat around talking and listening to records. While one of the records was playing I noticed Tommy tapping along to it. I just happened to mention in passing that he seemed to have rhythm and that if he bought a kit of drums I would teach him how to play. I never thought any more about it until two days later when he came into work and said he had borrowed the money off his father-in-law and bought a drum-kit; was I prepared to teach him? I must admit I was quite taken aback with Tommy's keenness. I told him I would, so I started to go up to his house and within a couple of weeks had taught him the rudiments of drumming. By this time Tommy and I had become quite close so I approached Stan Moores and asked him if he wanted to start a trio, with him on the piano, Tommy on drums and me singing. He said he was very interested and would give it a go. I then approached Tommy and told him that I had decided to start a trio with him as the drummer. Tommy was overjoyed, so we all got together and started rehearsing at the local working men's club. We hadn't got a name so we decided to call ourselves the Stan Moores Trio! And that was the humble start of Cannon and Ball's career.

If I had known the heartaches it was about to bring me, I might have stayed a drummer in the little working men's club. We rehearsed every Wednesday and slowly we got better and better, but the gigs didn't seem to come. We occasionally did the odd wedding but we weren't doing anything to set the world alight. I did more gigs when I was on my own. The only good thing to come out of it all was that I heard Tommy singing. So we decided to change the act so that Tommy would sing a couple of songs with me on the drums and then we would swop over and I would sing a couple. It seemed to work because a local pub named the Fitton Arms asked us if we would do every Sunday night. We were only too delighted. We stayed there for about two months, getting better all the time. Then one day Stan came in and said he had been offered a residency at another club and he felt he had to take it. We told him we understood and we parted the best of friends.

This left Tommy and me on our own. We decided not to get another pianist but to go out as a singing double act. We got as many songs together as we knew and started to rehearse them at Tommy's house. After a while we felt we were quite good (though looking back on it, we were rubbish). We set off on the usual rounds doing auditions anywhere and for anybody. We hadn't got a name for the act yet, so we bantered names around and finally I came up with what must be the worst name in the world for an act. Bobby and Stevie Rhythm! I told you it was bad. But at the time we thought it was wonderful. We were so excited to be a double act that we decided we must look like professionals. So off we went to Burton's the tailors and bought two sets of grey slacks and blazers on hire purchase. We took them home and we had two badges made, one for Tommy and one for me. There is a story about the badges. It was my brain-wave again and as usual it turned out all wrong. I had the idea that we should each wear a badge sewn on to our blazers, mine with BR written on it, meaning Bobby Rhythm, and Tommy's badge would have SR, standing for Stevie Rhythm. We had this done and we felt a million dollars. That week we had an audition at a local working men's club so we set off with our new stage clothes in a suit bag. When we arrived at the club we got changed into our new clothes and went to the bar for a drink. We hadn't even got up to sing yet when a woman came up to Tommy, looked at his badge on his blazer and said, in the loudest voice you have ever heard, 'Do you work for the SR toothpaste company?'

Poor Tommy didn't know where to look, he felt very embarrassed. She then looked at my badge, but before she could open her mouth I said, 'Before you open your mouth, no! I do not work for British Rail. We are a double act, Bobby and Stevie Rhythm. And we are singing here tonight.'

'Well,' she replied, looking us over with disapproval, 'I hope you sing better than you are dressed.'

I think that was the first and the last time Tommy and I wore those outfits. After that episode we also decided a change of name wouldn't do us any harm, so we changed it to the Sherrell Bros (after the Sherrells, a very popular Tamla Motown group). I agree it wasn't much better, but at least we wouldn't keep getting asked if we worked for a toothpaste company or British Rail. Later we became the Harper Brothers.

We carried on working at the factory as usual, while at weekends we would go around different places auditioning. Slowly our diary got fuller as we got more bookings, and eventually we stopped auditioning.

At work I was still a bit of a rebel, and one day things didn't turn out exactly as I'd planned. We had all started work as usual this particular morning and everything seemed normal. But it was winter and it was quite cold in the factory, and I thought it wasn't fair to us to be working in cold conditions so I decided to do something about it. (The truth was I felt rather bored and wanted something different to happen.) I approached Terry Brierly and told him that we shouldn't be working in these cold conditions. He agreed and asked me what we could do about it, so I told him that we should approach the management and tell them that either they put some heating on or we would all walk out. He suggested that I spread the word around the lads and if they were all with us that's what we would do. I immediately started going around the factory finding out who was with us and who wasn't. To my surprise everybody was with us.

The only one I hadn't told was Tommy. I arrived at Tommy's workbench and told him our plans. He told me that he would do what everybody else was doing. So now it was all stations go! Inside I felt very excited because now we could get our own back on the foremen and the manager, a fellow called Jack Moores who I thought had never liked me, maybe he did but I always felt that he didn't. (And it gave me a perverted sense of revenge when years later I offered him a lift to work in my Rolls-Royce!)

When the morning break came we all crowded into the canteen and started to discuss our plan of attack. It was decided that after our morning break we should go back into the factory and put down tools. This was very exciting for me, this was really rebellion. After the break we all went into the factory and put down our tools, then stood around talking. It wasn't long before Jack Moores and his team of foremen came down on to the shop floor. He stood on a packing case and we all gathered around him. He then proceeded to ask us what was going on. Everybody looked at me to answer and I in turn looked at Tommy. (Remember Tommy had nothing really to do with this, he was just going along with everybody else.) But as Tommy has done all his life, he took control. He told Jack Moores that it was too cold to work and unless the management turned some heating on it had been decided that we would all go on strike. Jack Moores looked at us all and told us that what we were doing was wrong and that we should work until dinner-time and then discuss the problem. Some of the men started to walk back to work like little sheep, but stopped when Tommy said that we would be prepared to work until dinner-time, but then after dinner, if the heating was still not on, we would all walk out. Jack Moores just laughed and walked off. We all went back to work determined to stick to our guns. Dinner-time came, we all had dinner then went back to the factory.

As we went into the building Jack Moores was standing with his foremen watching us. We all clocked on and felt that it was as cold as before. All the lads looked at me again and once again I in turn looked at Tommy. Tommy asked Jack Moores if he had turned the heating on. He told us all in no uncertain terms that he hadn't and that he had no intention of doing so and if we didn't like it we knew what to do. This was what I was waiting for. I made my way to the clocking-out clock with Tommy and the lads behind me. We clocked out one by one and walked out through the door. When we got outside there were only six of us. I looked back into the factory and all the other lads had given in and started work again. Out of a hundred men only six of us had gone on strike. There were Tommy, Terry Brierly, Ronnie Ravey, Eric Mullins, Jack Minton and myself. We all knew in our hearts that this would mean the sack. Well, we thought there was nothing for it but to go to the pub. (That always seemed to be the answer.) Later that night and a couple of pints heavier I arrived home and told Joan what had happened, hastening to add that all the other men had been cowards and the six of us heroes. She listened patiently and said I would have to find another job because now I had a family to keep. A couple of days went by and I received a letter. I saw the name of the factory on the envelope and knew that this was a letter telling me that I was sacked. Much to my surprise when I opened the letter, they were asking me to go back, along with the other five who had walked out. They also wrote that there would be no repercussions over what had happened. This was great news. We felt that we had won.

The next morning we went back to work feeling like heroes. We had fought the system and won. What fools we were, because two days later Tommy was called into the manager's office and fired. He was told that he had been the ringleader of the strike, and that they didn't want any troublemakers at their factory. I felt really guilty because I had been the one who started the trouble and all that Tommy had done was to voice our opinions. I tried telling the management this but to no avail, they were adamant, Tommy had to go.

Tommy left and before long all the ringleaders including myself had left. This didn't break up the friendship we had, quite the contrary. Tommy, Terry Brierly, Ronnie Ravey and myself would always for some reason or another find ourselves working at the same engineering works. So our friendship grew. We continued working the clubs at night and working as welders during the day. There was only one bad time for me during that time. I was out of a job and was having difficulty finding another one. It was coming up to Christmas and I needed money to buy our Robert some presents. I saw a job advertised in the paper for coal baggers. Beggars couldn't be choosers so I phoned them up and they told me to go along and I could have the job. The only drawback was that it meant working nights, but I wasn't bothered, I was happy to have any job. The snow was on the ground when I arrived at this old factory. It was a run-down old place with no windows. Obviously there would be no heating, but I wouldn't be striking this time, I needed the money too much.

I walked inside the building and couldn't believe my eyes. About twenty men stood there all waiting to start work. I looked at the men and noticed that most of them were the local villains and hard cases from around Oldham. I felt a little bit out of my league. But at least I had a job. The foreman came over to us all and pointed to some huge mounds of coal and told us to pick someone to work with, and then said that we weren't getting a wage but would be paid by how much coal we bagged. Some of the men walked out, but not me, this was a lifeline to me, at least I would be taking a wage home every week, I thought. This other man and I got two shovels and walked over to the biggest mound of coal we could find and started to work like demons possessed. We worked all through the night without a break, bagging one bag of coal after another. By the morning my arms felt as if they had been tied to the *Titanic*.

Morning came and the foreman said we could stop work. He told us to gather around him as he had something to say. He then proceeded to tell us that we had worked so hard that they had enough bags of coal to last them three months and they wouldn't need us any more, so he was sacking us. My heart felt it was going to drop out of my shoes. There I was, a tradesman with a young child, and no job. I felt that my life couldn't get any worse. But believe you me, it did.

The foreman paid us what we had earned that night and we all left. I walked home that morning with three pounds in my pocket, wondering what I was going to tell Joan. I had been ripped off and there was nothing I could do about it.

Someone must have been looking out for me again, because the day after, Terry Brierly came to our house and told me he had been offered a job as foreman at an engineering firm. He was getting the lads back together again. Tommy, Ronnie Ravey and I started work at this place and it felt good to be back at my old trade. By this time Tommy and I had become quite a decent act, and we used to work every weekend.

One day we were working in the factory when my cousin Wally Harper walked in. He looked at Tommy and me, and told us we were crackers working in all the smoke and grime when we could make more money as professionals. We told him that we had young families and that going professional was too big a risk. The following weekend was a bank holiday and he told us that he could get us good money for the Friday, Saturday, Sunday and Monday in South Wales doing the social clubs. We replied that if we worked the weekend in the factory we could get double time which meant more money, so it wasn't worth our while. He then told us that all our food and accommodation would be provided as well.

We thought this over and realised that if everything went to plan we would get a lot more than working in the factory. So we told him we would do it. We planned excuses to give the foreman as to why we would not be in work and got ready for the big weekend. It would be the first time that Tommy and I would have been out of Oldham with the act, and the first of many times that I was to be away from home.

Tommy and I set off on our adventure to South Wales feeling we were entering the twilight zone. In a way we were. We arrived at a little village just outside Swansea, and asked Wally to take us to our hotel as we were feeling tired. I should have known then that something was wrong, because Wally's eyes hit the ground. Tommy must have noticed it too, because he became suspicious. He asked Wally if he definitely had got somewhere for us to stay. Wally replied that he had and proceeded to take us up into the mountains. We seemed to be going for hours when suddenly we found ourselves in a field at the top of the mountain. At the bottom of the field were two tents. Suddenly out of one of the tents four children came running to greet us, and I recognised them as Wally's children. So that's why we had come here, I thought to myself, to see Wally's children. How wrong I was. After we had played with the children for a while Tommy asked Wally to take us to our hotel now as it was getting dark. Then Wally hit us with the bombshell. We didn't have a hotel, he told us, the other tent was ours. I couldn't believe my ears. Tommy proceeded to give Wally an ear-bashing but there was nothing we could do about it, because we didn't have any money until we had done the first gig. But we agreed that as soon as we had some money we would move into a hotel. Wally tried to make his peace by telling us that he would provide the food.

He was a lovable rogue and we found it hard to be annoyed with him for long.

Wally left saying he would bring us breakfast and Tommy and I went to look at the tent that we would be spending the night in. One look inside and we knew there would be no way we would be sleeping in that, it was smelly and dirty; it was so bad that a bedouin's sheep would have refused to shelter in it. So Tommy and I decided we would sleep in the car for the night. We settled ourselves in, Tommy in the front seat and me in the back. We talked until the early hours about families and things and then drifted off to sleep. Morning soon came with Wally waking us, shouting breakfast. When we saw what he had brought us, we couldn't believe our eyes. He had brought us bananas and morning coffee biscuits for breakfast. (Boy, this was living, and Joan thought I must have been having a good time.) It was pointless arguing with Wally so we just accepted the situation and ate our bananas.

The night came and we set off to do our first club in South Wales. It was situated in one of the valleys miles from anywhere. I didn't know that Wales had that many mountains. We eventually arrived and told the committee who we were, and they told us that we would have to do three spots (that means we would have to perform three different acts). We said okay and sat in the dressing-room, waiting to go on. The time came and we went on. We thought we had done all right, but obviously we were wrong, because when we came off the committee were waiting for us. They told us in no uncertain terms that we were rubbish and that we were the worst act they had ever had at the club. It was the first time that Tommy and I had ever experienced anything like this. Back in Oldham, when we did the clubs we always took a few of our mates with us, so we always went down well. But this was different, because now we were on our own.

We felt devastated. The committee gave us a couple of

pounds for the spot we had just done and told us to get
out. Our pride shattered, we packed our stage suits into
our bags and crept out of the club with our tails between
our legs. Everybody in the club was looking at us and we
felt as if we had committed a murder or something. I
don't think Tommy and I spoke for the next couple of
hours, we were too dumbstruck. We had only made a
couple of pounds so any thought of a hotel was out, so we
got into the car and made a silent journey back to our
bedouin tent on the top of the mountain. So much for our
first performance in South Wales. Tommy (always the
optimist) said it would get better. How wrong he was, it
only got worse.

The next day Wally came and asked how we had done,
we told him what had happened and he told us that every
act has to be paid off (as he called it) to be able to call
themselves pros. I quickly told him that's all right for
pros but we weren't pros. That night we set off for the
second club in South Wales and the same thing happened.
We were paid off again. This was getting ridiculous.
Slowly all the confidence we had was beginning to slip
away. This happened at every club we did that weekend
except for the Sunday dinner-time show and we managed
to last that one out. So out of the five clubs we had come
down to do, we got paid off at four of them. Maybe instead
of being called the Sherrell Bros we should have called
ourselves the Paid-off Bros.

The long weekend was over and Tommy and I gladly
set off for home. On the long journey back to Oldham we
talked about packing it all in. We were going home with
twelve pounds in our pockets, which was ten pounds less
than we had set out with. We may have talked about
packing it in but deep in our hearts we knew we wouldn't,
because we loved it, even when it was this bad. But it
would be a long time before we went back to South Wales.
We did go back many times through the years, but that
memory will stay with Tommy and me for ever. And

funnily enough South Wales is now one of our favourite places in Great Britain to work. Back at work we lied and told our mates that we had done well and that they wanted us to go back and perform at a future date. (If only they'd known the truth.)

On the home front everything seemed to be going fine. Robert had grown up a little and had become a regular little mate. Tommy and I continued working at the factory and doing the pubs and clubs at weekends. But looking back I realise that Joan wasn't seeing a lot of me and it would only get worse. Maybe our marriage had started to crumble even then but neither of us realised it. The cracks would soon start to appear over the next few years as I invested more and more time in my dream of becoming a star, while our domestic life came under an increasing strain.

4

The professionals

Looking back the turning point in my career happened one Friday night in a club in Stockport in Cheshire. As usual Tommy and I were having our Friday night out with the boys and we had decided to go to this club. I did not realise that what would happen that night would change my lifestyle for ever. When we arrived at the club it was packed, but we managed to find a seat in the corner. We got our pints of beer and sat back to watch the acts that were performing there that night. After a couple of pints some of the lads started suggesting that Tommy and I got up on the stage because we were better than the acts that were booked there. We weren't really, but thankfully our mates thought we were. (To tell you the truth if they hadn't put us forward, we would have volunteered anyway. We were that modest!) Terry Brierly approached the man in charge and told him that he had two mates with him who wanted to get up and sing. The man in charge was very gracious and told Terry that we could get up after the girl singer who was on. Terry came back and told us what the man had said. Tommy and I got very excited because this was a night-club and not the usual working men's clubs that we were used to. When the time came we went on stage and proceeded to storm them, left them shouting for more and went back to our seats. We knew we had done well when the man in charge of the club came over and asked if we would return as a paid act. We sat there for a while basking in our glory, when a man at the far side of the room beckoned us over. We went, thinking that maybe he was a booker from another club who wanted to book us. How wrong we were! When we reached his table we could tell he was more than just a club booker. He was wearing a mohair suit and had a gold watch on and gold cuff-links on his shirt. To us this was a man of wealth. He proceeded to tell us that he was a professional manager from London. He thought we had talent and he wanted to manage us. Tommy and I told him that we weren't professional, but semi-professional, and that we had families to look after. We just sat there open-mouthed as he told us he would like us to go to London to his offices, sign a contract, then go back to work, resign and become fully-fledged professionals. He promised that we would have far more work than we could ever imagine. Tommy and I went back to our table unable to speak, we were floating, this was a dream come true, it was like something you only see in movies. We told the lads what he had said and they were glad for us, so we celebrated by having a few more pints. I went home and told Joan. I don't think she realised what it meant, but she never stood in my way. The next day Tommy and I discussed what had happened and decided to give it a go. We figured that if it didn't work out we could always go back to welding.

We took a day off and went down to London to sign the contract. It was a big day for Tommy and me, because we had never been to London before and we felt we were going to be stars. We signed the contract, had a little look around London then set off back to Oldham with our heads in the clouds.

We went to work and told them that we were resigning

because we were turning professional. They wished us the best of luck and Tommy and I set off into the unknown world of show business. We had high hopes, but in fact this was going to be the start of the most miserable two years of my life.

Dreams are meant to be shattered, and our dream was no different. Our new manager's promises of fame and work turned out to be hot air. The only work he found us in twelve months was a weekend in Newcastle. Because we had no work, times started to get hard, but Tommy and I decided to stick it out as long as possible to see if we could make it as pros. Joan was working, so at least we had a bit of money coming in, but it wasn't enough to pay our bills. But this didn't seem to matter, for some reason I just put this to the back of my mind and carried on living my dream.

We started to find small jobs, such as putting someone's loose slates back on their roof, or building little garden walls. We did anything to survive. But the sad thing was I didn't survive. I got so far behind in my mortgage repayments that I started to receive letters from the building society telling me that they were going to repossess the house. There was one time that I will never forget. There were Tommy and I, these two so-called professional entertainers, with not a penny in our pockets and not knowing where our next loaf of bread was coming from, seated on someone's roof in the middle of a blizzard putting slates back on. I can still see it now. I told Tommy all my troubles, and told him this show business lark wasn't working out and that we should get a job. I will never forget Tommy's optimism. He just listened to me and then told me quietly, with all the confidence in the world, that this was just the start, and that we couldn't get any lower than this, so the only way was up. He managed to take away my fears, and before we knew where we were, we were laughing as if we didn't have a care in the world. All our life, when things got rough,

Tommy has always tried to keep my spirits up. And I thank him for this, because without his confidence and optimism I'm sure I would have given up many times.

During these hard times Tommy managed to get a part-time job from a friend of his who had dog kennels. He told me that if I wanted to help him he would give me half his wages. He didn't have to ask twice. Thinking back on it there was not a lot for me to do, so I realise that Tommy was just trying to help me out. We used to get to the kennels about ten o'clock in the morning, clean them out and then spend the rest of the day talking and dreaming about when we would hit the big time. It was not to come for a long time yet and there was to be a lot of heartache along the way. We even went for an audition for a popular television programme called *Opportunity Knocks* and were told that they would be in touch with us. We thought that meant we had failed.

Things got so bad that Joan and I had to approach money lenders to try to get ourselves out of debt. What we didn't realise was that it made things worse. We had to pay them back at such astronomical rates that we just plunged further and further into debt. We knew when the debt collectors were going to arrive, so when they were due Joan and I would turn off all the lights in the house and hide under the window until they had gone. Many times I have had to put my hand over our Robert's mouth to stop him shouting at the wrong time. I can still see them now trying to peer through the window to see if we were in. The money lender started to get very nasty, threatening Joan and me that he would take us to court. This didn't bother me as I already had quite a few court orders against me. What did bother me was that I was getting more and more behind with my mortgage payments, and with having to pay the money lender back there was no way I was ever going to get out of the hole I was in. One day our Sylvia arrived and saw that I was sad. Before long I was blurting out the whole story to

her about the money lender and everything. She listened
patiently then asked me what day the money lender came
to collect his money. I told her he came on Fridays.

She told me not to worry, everything was going to be
all right. Our Sylvia was always like that, nothing ever
seemed to worry her, she went through life like a tornado.
Friday came and suddenly the door-bell rang. I started
to panic, I thought the money lender had come early. I
quickly switched off all the lights and darted under the
window. Joan and I sat there with our Robert in our arms
not daring to breathe. Then I heard our Sylvia calling
me from outside.

'Robert, it's me,' she shouted.

I let her in, feeling rather stupid, and told her I had
thought it was the money lender who had come early.
She didn't say anything but just laughed. I asked why
she had come and she told me she had come to see the
money lender. Now I started to worry again because I
knew our Sylvia would argue with anybody. She calmed
my fears and told me that she had a proposition to put
to him. I asked her what it was but she wouldn't tell me.

The time approached for the money lender to arrive
and we all just sat there in silence. Suddenly the door-bell
rang and I knew it was him. I let him in feeling very
small. Here was a man with a lot of money who had a
hold over me. Humiliation hung over me like a cloak. He
came in and just looked at me. I told him that I had no
money to pay my debt but if he could give me longer to
pay I would give him a pound a week until I had paid it
off. He looked at me as though I was scum and told me
in no uncertain terms that this was not good enough.
Suddenly our Sylvia, who up to this point had said
nothing, told him that I wasn't going to pay him a pound
a week, in fact I wasn't going to pay him back any of the
money that I owed him. There was silence in the room.
I thought our Sylvia had gone off her head. The money
lender looked at her and demanded to know who she was.

She told him that she was my sister and that she had
done some checking up on his business. He told her that
he would take me to court and take everything I owned.
Our Sylvia, who was only four foot nine, walked across
the room to the money lender and stood there looking up
at him. She told him that she had found out that he was
an illegal money lender and that I had already paid back
twice the amount that I had borrowed in the first place.
She went on to say that she knew he hadn't paid any
income tax on his illegal profits and that if he didn't get
out of the house now she would phone the police and have
him arrested for harassment. He turned purple, but there
was nothing he could do. Our Sylvia was right. He turned
on his heel and left the house, slamming the door. It was
amazing that within the space of ten minutes our Sylvia
had taken away a nightmare that I thought I would never
be rid of. Our Sylvia was always like that, always there
whenever we needed her. But sadly she wasn't to be with
us for much longer.

My troubles were far from over. The building society
was by this time getting very insistent about my loan,
demanding that I did something about my back payments. Joan and I talked and decided that it was no use,
we would just have to let them repossess the house. I
wrote them a letter explaining that I couldn't pay and
asking if they would take the house from us. They said
they would and Joan and I moved into a council house
in what was then one of the roughest estates in Oldham.
It was called Sholver estate. Today after only thirty years
all the houses are derelict and boarded up.

During all these troubles one thing happened that
brought a little sunshine into our lives. We had a second
child, another boy. We named him Darren. So now our
Robert had a brother and I had two sons.

Months went by and our career started to take off.
We started getting bookings at clubs up and down the
country. Ten days in Scotland, ten days in the north-east,

ten days in South Wales. Slowly our diary was getting quite full. The only drawback to this was that I was spending more and more time away from home, and my marriage was beginning to come apart at the seams. But I was so full of myself that like the fool I was I didn't even notice my marriage crumbling around me. I'm still surprised that Joan stuck in there as long as she did.

Tommy and I by this time were fully-fledged pros. We had given up the job at the dog kennels and now made our living just by singing. One day Tommy came down to our house very excited. He had just received a letter from the TV programme *Opportunity Knocks* telling us that we had passed the audition and that they would be in touch with us when they wanted us to appear on the programme. (If you don't remember it, *Opportunity Knocks* was a kind of talent show.) This was great news for Tommy and me, we thought that before long we would be stars. What foolish men we were! More was to happen in the next twelve months of my life than I could ever have conceived.

I went round like a madman telling all my family and friends that I was going to go on television and that maybe I was going to be a star. They must have thought I was crazy. While my head was in the stars my world was crashing down around me. But something good did happen to me during that time and changed my life for ever. We had a booking in the north-east for ten days so we packed our bags, kissed the wives and children good-bye and set off to make some money, but more import-antly to have a lot of fun.

We had just finished working at a club in the north-east when a man came up to us and said there was a party going on down the road and asked us if we would like to go. Would we like to go? Was the man crazy? There was no way he could have stopped us. Before we knew what had happened we were smack bang in the middle of the party. This looked like being a great night. The beer was flowing freely and there were plenty of women about. At that time to me this was perfect happiness. (Now I realise that the only true happiness anyone can have is finding Jesus and the truth. Luckily for me Jesus already had his eye on me.) Suddenly the door burst open and in walked the most beautiful and fascinating girl I have ever seen. She stood about five foot ten, wearing thigh-length boots and a mini-skirt that showed the longest legs I have ever seen. Over the top of this she wore an old fur coat that came down to her knees, and her hair was something else. It was dark in a type of page-boy style, but what made it different was that she had one blonde streak running all the way down one side of it. This was never done in those days and she stood out like a lighthouse on a foggy night. With her height she had an arrogance about her and she knew that everyone was looking at her. But what gave her away were her eyes, the saddest eyes I had ever seen. I was to find out later on in life that the arrogance was only a cover-up for the most loving, gentle person anyone could wish to meet. Little did I know the way that our future lives were bound up together. (Forgive me for explaining what she was like but at this moment I am just enjoying my memories.)

She was with another man that night so I knew there was no chance for me, and besides she was five foot ten and I was only five foot four and a quarter (don't laugh, when you're only five foot four the quarter matters). Tommy and I left the party in the early hours of the morning feeling quite the worse for wear owing to the amount we'd drunk, and made our way back to our digs. It wasn't going to be long before I saw the tall lady again. Two days later there was another party and Tommy and I were two of the first people to be there. I found the only armchair in the house and parked myself in it. By this time I had started to drink so I had brought a crate of Newcastle Brown ale with me. I put this beside my armchair, so now that I had my drink and my armchair I settled back to play my favourite game of people-watching. This is a game that doesn't take much energy, all one has to do is to keep quiet and watch other people all the time. It's amazing what you see. The party had been in full swing for about an hour when who should waltz in but my tall lady. This night she was with a girlfriend. I watched for about ten minutes, then decided that tonight was the night I was going to knock a bit of arrogance out of her. Having the only armchair in the place with everybody else sitting on the floor, I had a great plan to get to talk to her.

She was standing just in front of me, so I stood up and tapped her on the shoulder. She turned round and looked down at me. She must have thought 'who is this little man' but she didn't say anything. I told her that I was going to the toilet and that she was not to sit in my chair or there would be trouble. I knew that what I had said would ruffle her feathers because I doubted that anyone had ever spoken to her like that before. I went to the toilet and when I returned, sure enough she was sitting in my chair. I didn't say anything but just looked at her, and to my surprise she got out of the chair and just smiled at me. I think she knew what I was trying to do. She was very charming, and told me that her name was Yvonne and that she was a waitress at the local nightclub. Maybe she was talking to me out of sympathy, but it didn't matter, at least she was talking to me. Anyway we spent the rest of the night together (just talking, I hasten to add).

I started to go off into a sort of Walter Mitty world, because for some reason I told her that I wasn't married and that I lived alone in a little flat in the centre of Oldham. I told her so many lies that I began to lose track of what I had said myself. The night passed quickly and before long the dawn arrived. Sadly for me we said our goodbyes and arranged to meet the following day.

I had been unfaithful before to Joan, but the other

women I had been with seemed to be only one-night stands. With Yvonne it seemed different. I never seemed to think of Joan's feelings, only my own, and I only seemed to worry over whether I would be caught or not.

I met Yvonne a few times during those ten days in the north-east and I was really enjoying her company, she made me feel at ease and the only drawback to this was our different heights. But it seemed to bother me more than it bothered her. On the last night of our run my lies caught up with me. I phoned Yvonne to see if I could meet her after our show, but she told me in no uncertain terms that it was impossible, because she said that I had lied to her. I tried to bluff my way out of it but it was no good, she knew. She told me I had taken her for a fool, and that she didn't go out with married men. She said I should go home and take care of my family instead of running around the country telling lies to everyone, then she asked me not to ring again. I put the phone down and felt I had lost something very special. But in my heart I knew she was right.

Tommy and I set off for home and our families. After about a week I was beginning to get itchy feet to be back on the road. But it wasn't too bad, because by this time Tommy and I were working on average three or four times a week. Joan had a job at a factory nearby, so during the day I would get Robert and Darren ready for school, and after seeing them off I would mess around all day waiting for them to come home. I would make Joan's tea ready for when she came home from work, and then about six thirty in the evening Tommy would pick me up and we would go to clubs all over Yorkshire, entertaining. I wouldn't arrive home until the early hours of the morning and by that time Joan would be in bed. This went on day after day, week after week, month after month. I was living a lifestyle that just wasn't suited to marriage.

Something happened during this time that left me with

a guilt complex I have lived with all my life. We had received a letter from *Opportunity Knocks* saying that we would be appearing on it in two weeks' time. Between the audition and being asked to appear nearly twelve months had passed. When we auditioned we were singers, but now we had become comedians. I know I say 'we became comedians' quite casually; well, I say it this way because that is how it actually happened, 'quite casually'. I noticed that comedians always got more money than singers; at that time I never understood why, but now I do. What I learned was that a singer can hide behind a song if things aren't going right, but a comedian has nowhere to hide. I think that's why in clubs in those days comedians always got more money than the singer. So one night I dropped a gag in between songs, and much to my surprise it got a laugh. Now I can tell you there is no feeling like it in the world when an audience laughs, particularly at a joke you have just told. Tommy enjoyed it too. So the next night I did the gag again and before we knew where we were we had become comedians. Not very good at the beginning I grant you, but then again to be a comedian is a craft that has to be learned.

Not only that but we had changed our names from the Harper Brothers to Cannon and Ball. We had now become a true double comedy act, with Tommy acting as the straight man and me as the comic. We felt that Tommy needed a strong name and as he had always liked an American singer named Freddy Cannon, we decided that he should call himself Tommy Cannon. Obviously to make our new name sound like a comedy act I was going to have to be called Ball. It took a lot of persuading on Tommy's part, but eventually I gave in and became Bobby Ball.

One night, about a week before we were due to go to London to record the show, I was getting ready to go out when the phone rang. It was our Sylvia, she was phoning to wish me good luck on *Opportunity Knocks* and she went on to say that she was feeling very depressed. I talked to her for a while, and in the conversation she told me she had taken an overdose of tablets. I wasn't overly worried by this as she had threatened to commit suicide many times before. I told her not to worry as I would come down to her house in the morning. I told her that I couldn't come now as I had a gig to do. She said it was all right and that she would see me in the morning. Tommy picked me up as usual and we went over to Yorkshire to do a club. I got home at about one o'clock in the morning. I was just going to bed when there was a knock on the door. I opened it and there stood my sister Mavis. Before she could speak I knew exactly what she was going to say.

'Our Sylvia's dead!' I said.

She just looked at me and asked how I knew. I told her about our Sylvia phoning me. She told me not to blame myself as she would have done exactly the same thing. But she couldn't understand the guilt that I was feeling, it weighed very heavily on my shoulders. It preyed on my mind that I could have saved her if only I had gone down to her house, but instead I did what I have done most of my life, I put show business before anything else. I give thanks to God that much later he came and took my guilt away. I carried that guilt, unknown to anyone, for twenty years. My parents took our Sylvia's death badly, they couldn't understand why she had done it. She was their first child, and to them she had always seemed bright and cheerful. What they didn't know was that she was always prone to fits of depression and at that time she was having a few personal problems. It must have got too much for her.

Tommy and I went down to London to record *Opportunity Knocks*. We thought we had done quite well, but we came last in the competition. In fact we were so bad that we had a few bookings cancelled. As for our dream of it making us stars, that would have to wait for another fifteen years.

A few months after our debut on TV something else happened that changed my life – my marriage split up. The marriage hadn't been good for a while, so I decided to do something about it. I decided to leave Joan for a couple of days so that she could see that our marriage was in trouble. My egotism was so complete that I thought if I left, Joan would come running after me (now, that's what I call being big-headed). I turned up late one evening on our Mavis's doorstep. She welcomed me with open arms and asked what the matter was, and I told her I had left Joan to try to teach her a lesson. Our Mavis asked me if I was doing the right thing and I told her yes, because Joan would come looking for me in a couple of days and then everything would be all right. Our Mavis lived in a little terraced house, it was a two up, two down, and had an outside toilet. She told me the only room she had was the back bedroom and her children were sleeping in it. She said that if I didn't mind sleeping with the children I was quite welcome to stay for as long as I wanted. I told her that sounded fine, so I settled in and waited for Joan to come and get me. One day passed and then another and then another. Before long a week had gone by and Joan had come nowhere near. Now, I was beginning to miss her and the kids, so I decided to go home and tell her I was coming back. When I arrived home I found she had changed the locks on the door, so I broke down the door and waited for her to come home from work. She eventually arrived and we settled down to have a talk to sort out our differences. Joan told me she didn't love me any more and that she didn't want me to come back. I have never felt so shocked and hurt in my life. My mind wouldn't let me believe what I was hearing. Surely Joan couldn't stop loving me just like that? Had I been a bad father? Maybe she didn't mean what she was saying? All these thoughts and many more kept rushing through my brain. But Joan explained that the old saying 'Absence makes the heart grow fonder' wasn't true in her case. With me always out and about rushing around the country, her love had gone cold. She now wanted me out of her life.

To separate from or divorce your wife must be one of the most horrendous things that any human being can go through. It strips you of all your dignity. It makes you feel a failure. The emotional pain is something that unless you go through it yourself, it is impossible to explain. It takes you into a world that you just don't understand, you have no security and you start to feel that you will never smile or love again. I had just lost our Sylvia and now I had lost my family. I was an emotional wreck. I don't want what I am writing to make Joan seem a very hard woman, because she is far from being that. She is a very caring woman and has been a wonderful mother to our two children. I take the blame for our marriage breaking up, it was I who took the love that Joan had and it was I who squandered it, and when it was too late I thought that she could just start loving me again. (I'm sorry for the pain I must have caused you, Joan.)

I went back to our Mavis's not knowing which way to turn, but in my heart I still believed that there might be a chance that she would take me back. I just couldn't stop crying, I kept going back and making a nuisance of myself, begging her to take me back. But it was not to be. I became what I will call a Sunday dad. If you look every Sunday in parks and zoos around the country, you will see men on their own with children. I guarantee that half of these men are Sunday dads who have custody of their children for the day. I would pick our Robert and Darren up on the Sunday morning and, just like all the Sunday dads around the world, we would go to a park or something, just so that we could be together. It would break my heart wondering what they thought of me, wondering if they really hated me for what had happened, or if I would eventually lose their love as they got older. Then I would take them home at the end of the day, hoping that Joan would ask me in.

During these terrible months Tommy would try to keep my spirits up. He would talk to me and tell me that it was about time I got on with my life and stopped looking to the past. But I couldn't see any light at the end of this long black tunnel I was in. Nothing seemed to matter.

We were due to go back to the north-east for another ten-day run, so Tommy suggested (to use his words) that I gave that tall girl I had met twelve months ago a ring to see if I could take her out, because he said I had got on well with her before.

I told him she wouldn't go out with me because I was married, and that she didn't like me any more because I had lied to her. And besides I wasn't sure if she would remember me or not. He told me to stop being so negative and at least give it a try.

'Who knows,' he said, 'she might make you laugh again.'

We arrived in the north-east, got settled in the digs and then after much thought I plucked up the courage to ring her. I could hear her phone ringing and my heart was thumping as if it was going to jump out of my chest. Eventually she answered.

'Hello?'

It was good to hear her voice again, all the memories of the ten days we spent together came flooding back to me.

'Hello,' I eventually replied.

'Who is it?'

It took me quite a while to answer, because I was not sure whether she would put the phone down or not.

'It's me. Bobby Harper.'

The line went dead for a moment, and I knew she couldn't remember me, or she was pretending not to. I decided to help her memory.

'You know,' I said, 'Bobby Harper. You'll remember me as one of the Harper Bros.'

'Oh yes!' she said, as if my name had just connected with her memory cells. 'The little man who tells lies.'

It was obvious that she hadn't forgotten. I tried to smooth things over.

'Yes,' I answered quickly. 'I was just wondering,' I continued, 'you see, I am working up here for a few days and I was wondering if you would like to go out for a meal or something?'

'I told you before, I don't go out with married men,' she replied, very tersely.

So that was my answer, there was no way she was going to go out with me. But I wasn't going to let her get away this time.

'But I am not married now,' I said. 'Well, I am married, but we have split up, so I am separated.'

It hadn't come out as I wanted it to, but at least it was the truth.

The line went quiet for a while and I could practically hear her brain working. Then she said, 'Okay then, I will meet you in the town about eight o'clock.'

I put the phone down and for the first time in many months I felt a little bit of happiness. I don't know whether she had agreed to meet me because she liked me or because she felt sorry for me, but it didn't matter, at least she was meeting me. It turned out to be the start of the most beautiful relationship between two people, that has lasted twenty-odd years. (I praise the Lord, Yvonne, for giving me the pleasure of your company all these years.)

That evening I met her and explained what had happened, and she just sat there and listened while I poured my heart out. When I had finished my tale of woe she just took my hand and told me that everything was going to be all right.

We got on like a house on fire. We saw each other every night after that and when it came time for me to go home, we found that we couldn't be apart. So that is when

I started what I call my two-hundred-mile courtship.
That means that four times a week I used to drive from
Oldham to Stockton-on-Tees, a round trip of two
hundred miles. But it was worth every minute on the
road. As Tommy had predicted, she taught me to laugh
again.

Our career was really starting to take off. We were
now doing nightclubs, and going down well wherever we
went. I remember one club we went to in Leeds, one of
many; Tommy and I had a double that night (that means
we had to do two clubs the same night). That particular
night was New Year's Eve. Tommy and I were a little
bit the worse for wear as we had already partaken of a
few drinks to celebrate the New Year. When we arrived
at the second club it was about eleven o'clock, and as we
went in the back door we saw a long dark corridor leading
to the stage. There in front of us was the figure of a man,
dressed in a top hat and a cape. He was just about to go
on, when I thought I would be friendly and wish him a
happy New Year. So I ran up to him and slapped him on
the back.

'Happy New Year!' I said, with a huge grin on my face.

His head shot round and he looked at me as if he
wanted to kill me. But he hadn't time because the compere had announced his name and he was already making
his way on stage. I realised then why he had looked at
me in that strange fashion. What I hadn't realised when
I slapped him on the back was that he was a magician.
It was only when I saw a few bird's feathers fall from
beneath his cloak as he walked on stage that I realised
that I had innocently hit one of the birds hidden within
his cloak. I just stood there watching with a macabre
sense of humour for a bird with a black eye, or even worse
a dead one, to fall from beneath his cloak. But I was
spared, they all seemed okay. It taught me a lesson, never
again would I go near anyone who was just about to go
on stage.

Another time I took Yvonne to a social club where Tommy and I were working that night. On the show was a guitar vocalist. We had just sat down when the concert chairman came over and told us to get ready because we were going on first. We went into the dressing-room and told him that we were comedians and that comedians as a rule in show business didn't open the show. He didn't seem to appreciate our giving him advice and told us in no uncertain terms that it was his decision and we were going on first. Tommy and I were by this time quite used to social clubs and people like him, who when they got on a committee and got a badge became power mad, so we knew it was a waste of time trying to change his mind. He was the boss and in his own mind he knew all about show business. He left us looking at one another, open-mouthed, in the dressing-room. We resigned ourselves to the fact that we would be going on first and proceeded to get changed. We had just taken our trousers off when he came back.

'No!' he said, in his broad north-east accent. 'I have decided you are right. I am going to put the guitar vocalist on first.'

He gave us a smile and left. Tommy and I looked at one another and felt that maybe he wasn't·so bad after all. We put our trousers on again and joined Yvonne at our table. She asked us what was wrong and I explained that the concert chairman didn't really know what he was doing but that everything was all right now. We had been sitting there for about five minutes when he came back.

'No!' he said. 'I was right in the first place. I want you two to go on first.'

Tommy and I got up like two schoolchildren and made our way to the dressing-room. We had just got our trousers off again when he came in.

'I've been thinking,' he said. 'Maybe you were right. I'll put the guitar vocalist on first.'

Tommy opened his mouth to speak but the man stopped him.

'Don't argue, lad,' he said. 'I've made up my mind and that's final.'

Tommy and I put our trousers back on and joined Yvonne again. This routine of coming and telling us that we were on and then we weren't went on for quite a while. After about the fourth time Tommy and I were getting really annoyed. He came again for the fifth time and told us that we were going on first. We went into the dressing-room and were just about to take our trousers off again when he came in.

'Hold it!' he said. 'The guitar vocalist had just told me he doesn't mind going on first so that's what we will do.'

'Is it?' Tommy said, looking at him full of anger. 'Well, I'll tell you what we will do,' he continued. 'My friend Bobby and I are not going on at all tonight, so you and your friend the guitar vocalist can entertain the audience yourselves.'

Tommy started packing our things away and the concert chairman just looked at me dumbfounded.

'What does he mean?' he asked eventually.

'He means,' I said, savouring the moment, 'that you can go on first and then you can put the guitar vocalist on, because we won't be here.'

He looked at us as if we had gone mad. It was obvious that nobody had spoken to him like this before, especially an act, who he must have thought he could treat like vermin.

'Do you mean you are refusing to go on?' he asked.

Tommy looked up from what he was doing and said, 'That's exactly what we mean. You can take your money and your club and shove it where the sun doesn't shine.'

Tommy always had a nice way of phrasing things.

'You can't do that,' the concert chairman said, his voice getting louder.

'Can't we?' answered Tommy, who by this time had the bit between his teeth. 'Just watch us. Come on, Bobby.'

We walked out of the dressing-room and started to make our way through the club.

The concert chairman came running out of the dressing-room like a man possessed.

'You will never work in show business again,' he shouted after us. 'I will report you to the agent.'

Tommy and I just turned round and smiled at him. This infuriated him even more.

'I'll tell all the clubs in the north-east,' he shouted. 'You'll never work up here again.'

By this time all the people in the club were looking at us. When they realised what was happening they started to turn nasty.

'Get out! We don't want you in the club,' a few started to shout, but Tommy and I kept on smiling. Suddenly I realised that we were walking down the opposite side of the club to where Yvonne was sitting. I looked across at her and could see that she was wondering what the hell was happening.

'Come on, love,' I shouted across the room. 'We're going to a proper club.'

This sent the people into fits of rage. But somehow we managed to get out. Once outside I told Yvonne the story and she laughed as I had never seen her laugh before. I realised then that not only was she a woman I found very attractive, but she was also a soul mate. Anyway we all went down the street laughing and headed for the Fiesta Club, to have some fun.

I remember the first time I met Yvonne's parents. Tommy and I were doing a social club one night and I arranged to meet Yvonne outside her house after the gig, and then we had decided to go to the Fiesta Club. When we finished the gig I arrived at her house only to find her standing at the window. She beckoned to me to go in so I assumed that her parents must be out. I went inside and she told me that she wasn't quite ready so I sat down on the couch to wait for her. Just then the door opened and in walked her mother. She looked at me and I stood up and shook her hand. I was feeling very embarrassed, I felt like a teenager again on his first date. We curtly said our hellos and then she asked Yvonne if she could see her for a couple of minutes in the kitchen. It all went quiet as they went into the kitchen, and I was wondering whether I was going to be thrown out at any moment. After a while Yvonne returned and we left. When we got outside I asked her what her mother had said. Yvonne told me her mother was shocked. She told me her mother had asked her if I was a Pakistani, because my skin was so dark, and why Yvonne wanted to go out with such a short man. That was my first meeting with the woman who was to become my mother-in-law. She has long ago realised that I am not a Pakistani and that I am the tallest in my family.

Yvonne and I decided to get married. But we had a problem. I told Yvonne I had no money and if she still wanted to marry me it would mean living at our Mavis's house in the back bedroom with two children. She told me she wasn't bothered as long as we could be together. Up until this time Yvonne hadn't met my family, so she decided one weekend she would come down to Shaw and meet everybody. Yvonne and our Mavis got on like a house on fire. I think our Mavis was pleased that Yvonne had brought some happiness into my life after all the pain I had been through. The next thing I had to do was to take Yvonne down to my parents' house and introduce her to them. She was petrified; she felt she was taking Joan's place and she had heard how my mother and father had liked Joan. When we got to my parents' house it took me a few minutes to coax her out of the car. I introduced her to them as the girl I was going to marry, and my mother made a fuss of her, saying, 'what a bonny lass' she was. My father didn't say much, but just kept looking at her. Eventually I asked him what he thought. He just looked at her, his eyes laughing.

'She's tall, isn't she,' he said.

'Yes,' I replied. 'What do you think of her?' feeling proud now, knowing that he liked her.

'She'll be all right for cleaning the windows,' he said.

Yvonne laughed, but there was a strange look in her eyes. When we got outside I asked her what was the matter.

'Don't think I'm being funny, Bob,' she said, 'but I didn't understand a word he said.'

'Why did you laugh then?' I asked.

'Because they might have thought I was ignorant if I didn't,' she replied.

Now it was my turn to laugh. I realised that she couldn't understand my father because he spoke in a broad Lancashire accent, and with Yvonne coming from the north-east it must have sounded total gibberish to her.

Yvonne and I got married on January 16th 1971 at the Oldham registry office. It was the biggest fiasco I have ever seen. The problem is that when I get nervous I start to laugh, and it is a problem that has got me into more trouble than I care to talk about. I even laugh at funerals. But this time was the worst of all. We stood in front of the registrar, Yvonne and I, with Tommy as my best man and all our guests stood behind us. The registrar was reading out the wedding vows when I felt myself starting to laugh. It was unbelievable, I could feel it starting and I tried to suppress it but it was no good. What made it worse was that Tommy had caught the laughing bug off me and he was starting to snigger. I have never felt so embarrassed in my life. I didn't want to laugh but I couldn't help it. The registrar was giving Tommy and me funny looks, but the more he looked, the more I laughed. I didn't want Yvonne to think I was laughing because I was marrying her. But my fears were unfounded because suddenly I could see Yvonne starting to giggle at the side of me. She had caught the laughing bug too. Before long it had spread around half the guests and they were trying to suppress their laughter. The registrar finally announced us man and wife and I am quite sure that he was glad to see the back of us. He must have thought we were crazy. We must have been because Yvonne and I had decided to get married on a day I was working; and not only was I working but I was doing two clubs that night. So it was arranged that Yvonne and all our guests would go to the second club, while Tommy and I would do the first club and meet them later at the second club after we had done our spot. Tommy and I arrived at the second club and saw all my wedding party waiting for me. We did our spot and joined them. But it was a strange feeling being on stage and seeing my wedding party in the audience; it felt as if Tommy and I were the cabaret that had been booked for the wedding. At the end of the night Yvonne and I went on our honeymoon, one night at the Royal George Hotel in Rochdale, which was about four miles away. It's ironic to think that even on our wedding night I left my wife; a way of life that I was to follow for the next twenty years.

We had our one-night honeymoon in Rochdale and then travelled the four miles back to our Mavis's and the back bedroom. It was wonderful of our Mavis and her husband Trevor to take us in like that. It was only a tiny house and Yvonne and I could never repay them for all the kindness they showed us. One would think with us all living together in such a tiny house that arguments would arise but in our case it was quite the contrary. We grew as a family and the love that was between us was a strong family love. Even today if any of us has a problem the family just drop everything they are doing to help each other out.

The back bedroom was so tiny that all we could fit in was a single bed. As Yvonne and I had no money we had to make do, so we slept on a single bed that was raised off the floor by four house bricks. Also in the room were bunk beds where our Mavis's children slept. One night I lay there with my arms around Yvonne thinking. I could hear the children sleeping deeply in the quietness that hung over the house. I could tell that Yvonne wasn't asleep, and I knew that she lay there thinking too, about what her future held.

I lay there thinking deep into the night, about how my life had turned out, about my two boys (oh, I thought a lot about my two boys), about Yvonne, how she had given up her life to come and live with me who had no money and no future, how she had left her family a hundred miles away to come and live with me in a back bedroom of a terraced house. I felt an overwhelming sense of hopelessness. As I lay there wallowing in my self-pity I began to get a different feeling, a feeling of confidence. At that time I didn't know what it was, now I know it was the Lord telling me that everything was going to be all right. I whispered Yvonne's name. She turned over to face me and I took hold of her hand, I told her that everything was going to be all right. I told her that some day I would buy her a big house, and that she would have so many clothes that she wouldn't know what to do with them, and I also told her that we would have a Rolls-Royce. She just patted my hand and told me in her maternal way not to worry and try to get some sleep. I could understand her, she must have thought I was dreaming. But I wasn't, I knew that the things I had said would come true. And they did. What I didn't know at the time was the pain that these things would bring, and that it was all part of the Lord's plan that would enable me to meet him.

5

The man from Oxfam

On May 15th 1972 Yvonne presented me with a baby, a girl, Joanne Patricia Harper. Now my family was complete, I had two boys and a girl. I continued to see the boys every Sunday and they were growing up into two fine lads.

By this time my career with Tommy was doing very well. We were out working nearly every night and had started to make a bit of money. Now Yvonne and I could start to think about getting a place of our own. We had a lot of difficulty in this area, we would find houses we liked but we couldn't get a mortgage because the building societies classed show business as a risk. (It's funny but when you become a star you are no longer classed a risk.) So we decided to get some rented property, and as we had no furniture of our own we had to get somewhere that was already furnished. We eventually found a house and settled in. It was great, now we were a real family with space of our own.

Things were going great for Tommy and me, we now had a manager, a man named Stuart Littlewood. He had managed us before but sacked us for not turning up at gigs. But now he had taken us on again, making us promise we would behave ourselves and work anywhere

he booked us. We told him we would and that our wild
days were over. If only he knew, they were just
beginning.

One day in about 1973 he phoned to tell us that he had
got us a summer season at the Carlton Hotel on the island
of Guernsey. (For anyone who doesn't know what a summer season is in show business terms, it means that an
act goes and works at a seaside resort for the whole summer. They are resident there and don't have to keep travelling up and down the country. A summer season could
mean at least twenty weeks' work.) We got very excited
at this news as it would be the first summer season that
we had done. The days seemed to pass slowly until the
summer came but eventually we set off. Yvonne and I
had rented a house in Guernsey and when we arrived at
the airport we made our way over to it. It was a big
place so we decided that Yvonne and I should live in the
upstairs part of the property and Tommy in the downstairs, and we would share the kitchen. When we had got
settled in Tommy and I headed for the Carlton Hotel,
where we found that it was a properly produced show
with other acts and dancers. This was quite new to
Tommy and me. We felt that at last we were really in
show business. On the bill were a magician named Sonny
Neil and a singing trio named the Song Spinners; top of
the bill was a tenor singer named Kevin Ross; and then
there were Tommy and me. Oh, and I mustn't forget the
dancers. This was going to be exciting. The season started
and Tommy and I were the second act on after the
magician.

We were doing all right, until one day when Harry (a
singer in the Song Spinners) and I were talking. He told
me I wasn't a real comic because we sang quite a lot of
songs (in those days Tommy and I would wear two nice
suits and do about two minutes cross-patter between
songs). What he had said preyed on my mind and I asked
what he meant and what we could do about it. He told

me that to be a real comic I should do something that would make the audience sit up and notice us as soon as we walked on. He even suggested that I should come from the audience to make my entrance. I realised that Harry was right. To be different from other comics I knew we had to do something quite outrageous.

I decided to make my entrance from the audience as an autograph-hunter wanting Tommy's autograph. The first thing I had to do was to get rid of my nice stage suit and buy something that would make people look at me. I told Tommy my idea and he agreed that we should try it. The next day we went into the town. We were just passing an Oxfam shop when I saw the ideal thing in the window. It was a large black evening suit. It must have fitted a twenty-stone man. It was much too large for me, but it was ideal. Tommy and I went into the shop and the man must have thought we were crazy when I said I wanted to try it on. I went into the changing booth and put the suit on. As soon as I put it on I knew I had found the real Bobby Ball. It felt good, I felt like a comic, it made me feel funny. I walked out of the changing room and Tommy started to laugh, then I knew it was right. He said what made him laugh was that the pants were so large that they hung in folds around my shoes. While we were in the shop we bought a large blue cummerbund, and the only other thing we needed were shoes. I spotted some old Hush Puppy boots in the corner so I said I would take them as well. Now I was ready. At last we had found me a character.

The evening came and we decided to try it out. Nothing like this was being done in show business so it was quite a new thing to try. I was going to make my entrance from the audience as an autograph-hunter so that meant I would have to sit in the audience before the show started. The room that we were working in was small, with tables and chairs spread around in front of the stage where people could watch the show and drink. Just before the show started I got changed into my new outfit and started to walk round to the front of the hotel. I could see all the people walking in and my nerve started to go. But I had come so far, so there was no turning back now. There I was, this little man in a huge baggy suit, with his hair parted down the middle, with brown Hush Puppy boots on, and to make matters worse I had an old Brownie camera hanging around my neck. I reasoned that no auto-graph-hunter worth his salt would be seen without his camera. I began to get second thoughts; this wasn't the show business I had been brought up to imagine. To me show business was all glamour, sequins and glitz, and there I was totally the opposite. I took a deep breath and prepared to 'die the death' (that's a show business term for being booed off). I began to walk towards the crowd of people going into the show. I started to get short of breath and I knew my adrenalin was working overtime because my bottom had gone tight. Before I knew it I was in among them. I started to act like one of them. I noticed people looking at me strangely. It felt quite good because I knew this idea might have a chance of working. I went into the room and found a table. I sat down and waited for the show to start. I could see people looking at me across the room. They thought I was somebody who was not a full shilling. I started to play my role to the full, ordering drinks from waiters and coughing loudly. I had the table to myself because everybody had avoided sitting near me. This was understandable.

I sat there for a while wondering whether I had made a mistake about this idea, when suddenly the lights went down and the curtains opened. The audience lost interest in me now and settled back to enjoy the show. In fact I started to enjoy it myself. It was the first time I had seen it from the audience's point of view. The dancers came on and then the magician. Then a voice from the back of the stage announced Tommy Cannon. I started to sweat, it was now or never. Tommy came on and started to sing a song. I let him get into about one line of the song and then I started to shout for his autograph and make my way to the stage. Tommy stopped singing and there was a deathly hush, the people believed that I was some kind of crackpot who was ruining the show. I got on stage with Tommy and looked at the audience. You could have heard a pin drop. They were just looking at me with their mouths wide open. The sweat started to roll down my back. Tommy and I went into the routine we had rehearsed.

I can understand people not laughing at the autograph routine but to Tommy and me it was original material. Allow me just a couple of moments to explain how the routine went. Tommy would be on stage acting as if he was a solo act, then I would come out of the audience, dressed in ill-fitting clothes. Then I would pretend that Tommy was my hero, so I would proceed to ask for his autograph, which Tommy would then give me, all the time I would be talking, saying things like:

'You are my favourite, Tommy, I've got all your records!' or,

'You're a leg-end to me, Tommy.'

Surprisingly these little sayings used to get laughs. Later on in our career the routine would sometimes backfire on us because we did it too well eventually. I would sometimes get thrown out of clubs, because people would complain that I was a nuisance and that they wanted to watch Tommy. They actually thought that I was an autograph-hunter. But once they found out I was part of the act, they would feel so stupid. And of course the act went down better once this happened.

It seemed we had been up there a thousand years when suddenly someone at the back of the room started to laugh. To this day I thank God for that person who started laughing. Before long all the audience were laughing. It felt wonderful. We came off and looked at one another, we were as high as kites. We knew that now we had done something original and not just a copy of all the other double acts. That night we became the Cannon and Ball act that would eventually bring us success.

We were having a great time that summer, we had a new act and my two boys Robert and Darren had joined us for a fortnight's holiday. Yvonne and I had decided that we needed a car to get us around the island, but we had no money so that was out of the question, until one day a friend said that he knew where there was an old banger for sale at twenty-five quid. I told Yvonne about it and she said she would manage for a week without any house-keeping so that I could have the car. I rushed around to where the car was for sale, very excited, only to find it was a clapped-out Ford Prefect. I asked the man if he would take any less for the car but he was adamant on the price. I paid him for the car and drove it away. On the way home I knew I had bought trouble because when I looked in my rear view mirror I couldn't see any cars behind me for smoke. There was so much smoke my car looked like a moving bonfire. It also didn't like hills, because when I got to a hill it couldn't get up it. I had to get out and get someone to help me push. But it didn't matter because I loved it. It had character. I still think about that car with fond memories. When I got home I showed it to Yvonne and she knew I had been ripped off, but she just smiled and said if I was happy that's all that mattered.

One day Yvonne and I and the kids were bored so I decided it was about time Ethel (that's what I had named my car) had a new coat of paint. I had found some old tins of paint in the garage at the back of the house so I knew it wouldn't cost us any money. I got all the kids together (Tommy's and mine), and asked them to pick a colour each. They looked at the tins of blue and red and yellow paint and their little eyes lit up. I then told them that they could paint the car. But I told them I didn't

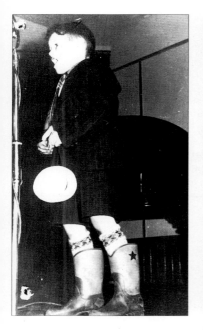

Top left: At the Lilac Nursery, aged about 5. The cowboy wellies were a Christmas present and I loved them!

Top right: The 'Bobby & Mavis' double act. My mouth was always that big!

Right: With my parents in 1959. I had just won the bookends in a holiday talent competition.

Left: This was the 'Black and Tans' - with my first wife Joan (right) in 1960.

Right: Yvonne and me with Joanne, when we were living in my sister's back bedroom.
(I've promised not to mention Yvonne's double chin - she'll kill me for that).

Right: Me and Tommy. If you notice - Tommy is the only one who can afford a jacket!

Below: A meeting with our hero Eric Morecambe.

Top: Celebrating my Birthday (and full of alcohol as usual) before I became a Christian.

Right: Another typical picture of me in the old days with an old friend Aiden J. Harvey.

Left: What can I say?
Can I get any better looking

Below:
With Gloria Hunniford on
one of our shows

Left: Tommy and me as we are now.
Old . . . old . . . old!

Right: Tommy and me as we were once - I'm about 28 here.

Above: One of the high-lights of our career - our first royal command performance, pictured here with Benny Hill.

Left: Smithy - the tramp I put in the Royal Box at The Dominion Theatre

Top: With my children - left to right, Joanne, Robert and Darren
Below: Yvonne, Joanne and me.

want it painted like an ordinary car, because this was a special car. I wanted it painted in pictures. I told them to paint whatever they wanted. I could tell they were excited so I left them to get on with it, telling them to let me know when they had done.

After about two hours our Robert came in and told me they had finished and asked if we wanted to look at Ethel. Did we? I couldn't wait! We went outside and Yvonne, Tommy and I just started to laugh. There stood all the kids covered from head to toe in paint. But what made us laugh more was what they had done to Ethel. She stood there looking like something just out of a nursery. She was covered in childish paintings. She had all their names written over her and there were pictures of clowns, dogs, cats, anything that a child would draw. She looked wonderful. I told them they had done a good job and gave them sixpence each. At least it had passed an afternoon for them. That night as I drove to the hotel I could see everybody turning open-mouthed to watch this backfiring, smoke-belching, multi-coloured machine come down the street. I couldn't help but laugh to myself, knowing that no one had ever seen anything like this on the sedate island of Guernsey. Ethel managed to cough and splutter her way through the season, and then a week before the season ended she coughed her last and died.

About three-quarters through the season disaster struck. I received a letter from the income tax people stating that I owed them money. Yvonne and I were devastated. Just as I thought I had got over my bad luck, here I was going back again to rock bottom. We talked it over and realised that there was no way that we had the money to pay them. Yvonne took control as usual. She sat me down on the settee, took hold of my hands and told me that after the summer season we would have to split up. I didn't know what to do. Before my eyes my new family was disintegrating. Oh, I was fine when it came to going on stage and showing myself off, but when

it came to real life I was hopeless. She must have seen
the panic in my eyes because she told me not to worry.
She said she would get her job back at home and I would
have to go back to our Mavis's and that while we were
apart we would save all the money we could and pay off
our debts. I loved her, the way she said 'our debts' when
she should have said 'your debts'. I realised that what
she was saying was that this was the only way out of the
mess I had got us into, so I unwillingly agreed. I wrote
a letter to the income tax people explaining that I would
pay them back so much a week and they agreed to this;
at least something was going my way. Yvonne and I got
through the rest of the season, but there was an air of
insecurity in our relationship.

The season ended on September 30th 1973 and my
daughter Joanne went with Yvonne back to her mother's
in the north-east, while I went back to the ever-faithfuls,
our Mavis's. It was a terrible feeling going back, it was
like starting all over again. But every week whatever
money I made I would take it up to Yvonne and she would
put her wage and my wage together and whatever we
had left after living expenses, she would use to pay my
debts off. Eventually after about a couple of months she
had managed to straighten me out, and for the first time
in my adult life I had no debts.

Now that I was in the clear it was time to get my
family back together and start again. We rented another
furnished house and Yvonne came back to Oldham to
join me. It felt wonderful to see my wife and daughter
again, to get up in the mornings and see them there. I
made a vow to myself that we would never split up again,
a vow that I broke time and time again.

I thought it was great to be living in rented houses
with no worry about mortgages and things, but I could
see that Yvonne wanted a house of her own. She knew
it was difficult to get a mortgage with me being in show
business, so she kept quiet and we just kept moving from

rented house to rented house. One day we went down to see my mother and father and across the road from them a building company had started to build a housing estate. On a huge hoarding in front of the building site the houses were being advertised for sale at £7000 each. This was pretty cheap for a new house in those days, as Yvonne quickly pointed out. Yvonne also pointed out that it was about time we bought a house of our own, but I argued with her that we were doing all right as we were, and that we didn't need the worry of a mortgage. She reasoned that instead of paying rent to someone to pay *their* mortgage off, we might as well use the rent money as mortgage payments on our own property. I agreed with her and told her to find out what the deposit was on the property. I thought that would keep her quiet because I knew that we didn't have enough money for a deposit. But I underestimated my wife's determination. She went out to the contractor's office to find out all the details. It wasn't long before she was back. I could tell by the look in her eyes that she was excited. She sat down and told me she had seen the main man and he had told her that there was no problem about me getting a mortgage, that they would get around that and also that the deposit was only £100. After she had told her exciting news she sat there looking at me expectantly. How could I refuse? Had she not given up everything and gone back home so that we could pay my debts off? I looked deep into her soft brown eyes, and they looked back at me pleading. There was no way I could have refused that woman. I told her I was willing to go for it if she was. She squealed with delight and gave me the biggest hug I have ever had in my life. This was to be the start of the fall and rise of Bobby Harper.

This was 1976, and 129 Harewood Road was the address of our new home. The contractor had shown us round and we were very excited. It was a three-bedroom semi-detached with gardens back and front. It was our first home. We didn't have any furniture, but this was only a minor problem. At last we had our own house. It was going to be about two months before we could move in because the builders hadn't finished the road and gardens yet, but that didn't matter. Yvonne and I had all the time in the world.

Our career at this time was doing pretty well, we were being booked quite regularly and everything was going great. One day our manager phoned to tell us he had got us six weeks in Australia, and that we would have to go in about a month's time. He gave us the date and it meant that I would be away when Yvonne and I were supposed to move into our new house. On one hand I was very excited about going, as neither Tommy nor I had been abroad before, and on the other hand I was a little bit worried about telling Yvonne because I knew how disappointed she would be. I plucked up the courage to tell her we would have to change the date of our move as I wouldn't be there, but there was no budging Yvonne, she was adamant that we were moving on the arranged date. I told her that I couldn't get out of Australia and she said that it was okay to go, as she would do it herself. So we left it at that.

I kissed Yvonne goodbye on the morning that Tommy and I were going to Australia, and set off for the airport to meet him. It was a wonderful experience. There we were, two ex-welders from Oldham, boarding a huge 747 to take us to the other side of the world. I sat back in my seat as the huge iron bird took off into the sky, and watched the ground disappear below me. It gave me a strange feeling. I had the feeling of stepping into the unknown. But it was a wonderful feeling. As I sat there thinking of Yvonne and the children they slowly drifted to somewhere at the back of my mind and I just started thinking of what the future would bring. During the flight Tommy and I were like two children in Disney World. What you must remember is that we had never been in a large aircraft before, so such things as the in-flight movie and the stewardesses with their trolleys full of free drinks were new to us. I have to tell you we felt a million dollars.

Eventually the plane landed in Sydney, and the agent met us at the airport. He took us to our hotel and told us we had three days off before we would be working, so this meant we had time to enjoy ourselves. We bade the agent farewell and walked into the hotel. We asked the porter for the keys to our rooms and he told us in his nicest hotel employee's voice that he only had one room booked for us. We didn't want to cause a fuss so we told him that would be quite adequate. He showed us to our 'room' and when Tommy and I saw it we couldn't believe our eyes. Outside the hotel had looked okay but inside it was a different kettle of fish. Allow me a few moments to describe the room. It was a small room and in the corner stood a grease-covered two-ring gas stove. (The porter told us that the hotel had no restaurant or room service and that if we wanted anything to eat we would have to make it ourselves.) In the room were two single beds and hanging over them were two almost black mos-quito nets, which had obviously never been washed from the day the hotel had bought them. I got the feeling that I had walked on to the set of some B movie set in the Amazon. At any minute, I expected a white hunter to walk in, but I was not to be that lucky. Standing against one wall was an old wardrobe that had seen better days; looking at it, it almost made me frightened to put my clothes in it. Hanging on the other wall was an old cup-board with all its paint peeling off it. The porter told us this was to put our food in when we bought some. Tommy and I just looked at one another as good as to say there would be no chance of that. And on the floor was a tatty old carpet full of holes.

We asked the porter in what district of Sydney our hotel was situated. He just smiled and said King's Cross and gave us a wink. We hadn't got a clue what the wink meant but we certainly found out later. Our hotel was slap bang in the middle of Sydney's red light district. It had an ominous reputation all over the world. Tommy and I had never heard of it before, but then again we wouldn't, coming from the back streets of Oldham. The porter just stood there with an 'I can get you anything you want' look on his face, waiting for us to tip him for his information. When we didn't, he gave us a very cross good-day. He didn't even say he hoped we enjoyed our stay, he just left, slamming the door behind him.

Tommy and I didn't speak for a moment, but just stood there dumbfounded. What had we got ourselves into? We threw our cases on the beds and sat down. We looked at one another and started to laugh. Here we were in the centre of Sydney, the sun was shining, we were alone on the other side of the world with an adventure before us; and we were feeling upset because we didn't have a nice room, and we weren't even paying for it. We laughed at the absurdity of it all. As we were unpacking I thought I saw something move under Tommy's bed. I looked again but I couldn't see anything, so I put it to the back of my mind, thinking it must have been my imagination. After we had finished unpacking we lay on the beds planning what we would be doing that night. For some reason I decided to have a look in the cupboard that was hanging on the wall. When I opened the doors I jumped back horrified at what I saw. There crawling about in the cupboard were dozens of cockroaches. I shouted to Tommy and he came running over. My skin began to crawl because I had never seen one before. Then I remembered a few moments before when I thought I had seen something moving under Tommy's bed. I told Tommy and we moved the beds away from the wall to check. I had been right! There were more under the beds, crawling over one another to escape. I hated them! They made me feel dirty! Tommy handled it much better than I could. Right away we went out and bought some cockroach killer. We sprayed the room and then went out to have a look around the shops while the spray did its job. When we got back all the cockroaches were dead, so we got to work and swept them all up. But for the rest of the six weeks we were there I couldn't go to sleep until I had checked that Tommy and I were alone.

We had a great time in Australia. We got to know people quite quickly, so that the six weeks we were there became a continual routine of lying in the sun all day and partying at night. I soon became accustomed to this way of life, and the more I became accustomed to it the further Yvonne and the kids slipped to the back of my mind. Money was a little tight, I was getting about £50 a week, so I would send Yvonne £12 and keep the rest for myself. Occasionally I would worry about how she was managing to make ends meet, but I didn't worry too much because I was beginning to get caught up in the 'me first before anybody else' syndrome.

On the last weekend before we were due to fly home the agent told us he had organised two concerts for four acts to entertain at a club in a mining town in the middle of the bush. It was arranged that we would all fly out in a small plane to the town, do the two concerts and then fly back again. The plane was so small that we all sat there facing one another. There were a double act called Macneal and Trotter, a comedian called Mike Harris, a woman singer named Ramona, and Tom and me. We knew the double act and the comedian, but we didn't know the woman, and as it was going to be a long weekend I decided I wasn't going to be lonely. So as soon as we had said our hellos and settled down I started to chat to the woman before anybody else could. She was in her late thirties and had an air of pomposity about her. She was a very striking woman, with a fantastic body. She was a little old for me at that time, but I reasoned to myself that as she was the only woman among us, beggars couldn't be choosers. She had ignored all of us, but I thought that was maybe because she was shy. She just sat there looking out of the window, as if we didn't exist. It was time to make my move.

I said hello, and she just looked at me, didn't answer, and then started looking out of the window again. Well I wasn't the type of person to be put off with a simple rebuff, so I tried again. I then asked her what her name was. She once again looked at me as if I was dirt under her feet and replied 'Ramona'. She then turned away and looked out of the window once again. This was getting beyond a joke. Tommy and all the other lads had stopped talking and were now watching this saga unfolding before their eyes. Well, there was no stopping me now. I was going to get her to say more than one word if it killed me. I then asked her what type of act she did, did she sing ballads or pop songs? I must have asked the right question because she slowly turned away from the window, raised one eyebrow and looked at me. I felt like a shrew trapped in front of a swaying snake.

'I,' she said, 'do not sing ballads or pop songs. I am a contralto singer. I am classically trained so therefore I sing songs from the classics. And I do not usually mix with variety acts.'

She then turned back towards the window, leaving me to sink further into my seat. This must have interested Tommy because he started to try to talk to her. But he did no better than me, all he got in reply to his questions were one-word answers.

Eventually he gave up, and all the other boys tried, but they received the same treatment. So we all left her alone.

When we arrived at the mining town I was amazed, it was like stepping into a cowboy film. It had one main dirt street, and I could imagine that when it rained it would turn into a quagmire. It had a board-walk with little shops running off it. We booked into a little rickety hotel and spent the rest of the time sleeping until it was time to go to the club. When we arrived at the club we were met by a huge Australian miner who told us he was in charge, and then he told us that the show we had to do that night would be a stag show, and the following night it would be mixed. We all said okay and went to the dressing-room. The club started to fill up and I took a peek through the curtains. Just looking made me sweat. The room was full of Australian miners, some of them had come direct from work and hadn't even had a wash. I could tell it was going to be a rough night because some of them were already drunk. I could see them swigging down their beer and throwing their heads back laughing. I ran into the dressing-room and told the other acts that we were in trouble because the audience looked more like a rabble than an audience. We all decided on a plan of attack. I told the comic who was the first act on to keep his material pretty clean because if we kept it clean the audience might come round to our way of thinking.

'No problem,' he said, 'I'll get them round to our way of thinking.'

The huge Australian came in and asked if we were ready. We told him we were and that the comic was going on first. The concert started and the comic went on. I couldn't believe my ears, he must have known every dirty joke in the book, not only was he swearing like a trooper, but he started to incite the audience, and they started to get rowdier and rowdier. Meanwhile backstage I could see the woman singer getting more and more nervous. My heart went out to her, because I knew that singing classical songs to a bunch of Australian miners let loose for the night, she was going to 'die the death'. So I made my way over to her and told her not to worry, and that if she was having a hard time to do just one song and come off, adding that we would cover for her. She just looked at me again with her eyes full of arrogance and said, 'I'll be fine.'

I just walked away disgusted. In my heart I was hoping
that she would 'die the death', just to take a little bit of
arrogance off her. The comic finished and then he introduced her. I couldn't wait to see this, so I went and sat
at the side of the stage. She went on with all the confidence in the world and started to sing 'I feel pretty' from
the musical *West Side Story*. The crowd went quiet for a
moment and then started to boo and cat-call her. This
didn't seem to bother her, she just carried on smiling and
singing her song. What she did next has never ceased to
amaze me to this day. She started to undo her dress. This
lady who had acted so high and mighty on the plane
was a stripper who sang. I couldn't believe my eyes, this
woman who had treated me like dirt was now undressing
in front of a load of beer-swilling miners. I wonder what
happened to her classical training? She finally stripped
off all her clothes, and by now the crowd was going wild.
I thought she would finish there, but no! I was wrong.
She carried on singing and walked off the stage and into
the midst of them. They started to paw her and do all
sorts of things but she carried on singing among it all.
This woman had some nerve. Towards the end of the song
she walked back on stage, finished the song and took a
bow, as though she had just finished singing an aria from
Tosca. I couldn't believe what I had seen. I rushed backstage to join the others, who were waiting to see what
type of attitude she would have now. It was unbelievable.
She just walked past us as if we didn't exist.

Because she was a stripper I forgot my experience on
the plane and thought I would try again, so I lied and
said I liked her act. She just gave me a look that would
make the Sahara Desert freeze over. I lowered my eyes
and walked away. But somewhere today in Australia
lives a stripper who sings the greatest 'I feel pretty' you
have ever heard.

The next thing I heard was our name being announced.
My nerves started to go because I knew that Tommy and

I had never been able to do dirty material, and tonight was going to be no exception. We went on and surprisingly the crowd seemed to warm to us. If it was because they had been satisfied by the stripper I don't know, but we started to do okay. We were getting laughs in the right places and we came off feeling really good. The night finished and all the acts, except the stripper, ended up in the bar. We started to crack jokes and discuss how we thought the night had gone. By this time in my life I had begun to enjoy alcohol, it made me feel different, it gave me a lot of confidence. And before the night was over I was well and truly drunk.

The following night came and we went to the club. The same miners who the previous night had been pawing and screaming over a stripper were tonight bringing their wives to see the show. I wonder if they had told them about the behaviour with the stripper. I guess not, men have a tendency to be cowards when it comes to that sort of thing. I was looking forward to it because I never liked stag shows even though Tommy and I had done lots of them in the past. For some reason they always left me feeling dirty and unclean. So with it being a mixed audience tonight, it was going to feel good to be able to do our act without having to worry if we were being dirty enough or not. Boy, was I in for a surprise! All the acts went on and did very well, even the stripper, who just sang that night. Then came our turn! We were announced and bounded on stage like an express train, ready to show the other acts just what Cannon and Ball were made of. We started the opening routine, and we must have been on stage for about ten minutes and we hadn't even got a laugh yet, I mean not a titter. The audience just looked at us as if we were from another planet. We could see the contempt in their eyes, we could feel a wave of hate hitting us. Inside I began to crumble, my shirt was wet through with sweat, and my top lip had begun to stick to my teeth (a sure sign of panic).

I looked at Tommy, and I could see that he was resenting what the audience were doing to us. Suddenly from the back of the room someone started a slow handclap, it spread like a grass fire, and before long everybody in the club was giving us a slow handclap. On top of this they started to shout 'Off! Off!' It was the most terrible feeling I have ever had. I stopped the act and looked at Tommy. He was just looking back at the audience with hate in his eyes.

'Let's get off,' I said, quietly.

Tommy looked at me for a moment and then said, 'No, Bobby!'

I couldn't believe what Tommy was saying, here we stood in front of an audience that hated us and there was Tommy saying that he was staying on.

He then turned back to the audience and shouted, 'So you don't like the act then, eh!'

This incited the audience even further, and they began to go berserk, shouting abuse and jeering. Now I could tell that Tommy was angry because he just sneered back at them. I just stood there wishing the ground would open up and kindly take me away. We just stood there for a few moments allowing all this abuse to hit us; every abuse that was shouted was like an arrow going through us.

Then Tommy shouted to the audience, 'You won't beat us. I had a dream last night.'

As soon as he said that I looked at him as if he had gone crazy. He had started the first line of a routine that lasted ten minutes. And he knew that if he gave a feed line I would have to give him the answer back. I just stood there astonished. He just smiled at me and gave the feed line again.

'I had a dream last night,' he said.

I knew he would stand there all night waiting for my line back if he had to, so I decided to give him the line back to get it over with. We stood there for the next ten minutes doing a routine that no one was listening to, they were too busy shouting abuse at us. Half way through the routine Tommy and I started to laugh and we ended the routine nearly on the floor. At the end of the routine Tommy looked at the audience.

'Thank you, ladies and gentlemen, for being such a different audience. I hope we never meet again.'

Tommy then put his arm around my shoulder and we took a bow as if we had taken them by storm. What the audience hadn't realised was that we were now taking the mickey out of them. We left the stage and when we got back to the dressing-room the other acts were too embarrassed to talk to us. But that didn't bother us. We just went to the bar on our own and got drunk.

The next day we went back to Sydney and caught the plane to England. On the plane I knew I had to get back to reality, by that I meant Yvonne and the kids. It wasn't going to be easy. For the past six weeks I had enjoyed being single again. I knew that I had sent Yvonne hardly any money, so I was wondering how she had managed. Funny how I never thought of that in Australia. She had moved into our new house on her own, we had no furniture or carpets, so I realised she must have had it rough. But I felt no remorse.

When we got back to Manchester Airport, Yvonne, Joanne and our Mavis were waiting for me. It was good to see them. Yvonne looked beautiful. I hugged and kissed her and then I took my daughter up into my arms and held her close. I didn't realise until that moment just how much I had missed them. I said my goodbyes to Tommy and set off for my new home. During the ride home I told Yvonne not to worry about furniture and things, that we would get them in time; she just looked at me and smiled. She then told me she had had to go into debt for some new clothes so that she could look nice for when I came home. Out of guilt I told her it was okay, she could have anything she wanted. We arrived at the

street that led to Harewood Road and when we turned
the corner I couldn't believe my eyes. There were banners
draped right across the road, saying 'Welcome Home
Bobby'. All the neighbours were at their front doors
cheering me. Now this was all strange to me because I
didn't know any of them, it was the first time I had been
to the house. What I hadn't realised was that Yvonne
had lived there for six weeks so she knew every one of
them. Even though I didn't know them it was a wonderful
gesture. We arrived outside our house and I got out of
the car, I waved to the neighbours and went inside. What
greeted my eyes was something that I will never forget
for the rest of my life. Yvonne stood to one side and let
me go in first. I expected to see an empty house but to
my surprise it was fully furnished. It looked beautiful. It
had a settee, armchairs, carpets and even a television. It
looked terrific, but I knew we were in trouble because we
didn't have the money to pay for all these things. I looked
at Yvonne and asked how much debt we were in. She
smiled and said none. I couldn't believe her. I sat her
down, took hold of her hands and told her not to be afraid
to tell me. She told me that with her family allowance
and the money I had sent her she had scrimped and
saved, even to the extent that she and Joanne had lived
on baked beans. So we didn't have any debt at all, everything was paid for. I broke down crying. I had never felt
so guilty in my life. Here was the woman that I had
married, scrimping and scraping to give me a nice home,
and there I had been in Australia, womanising and drinking and just thinking of myself. I loved that woman and
at that moment I felt that I was too big a rat to be in the
same room as her. She took hold of me and loved me as
a mother would love a baby. I promised that somehow I
would make it up to her, but it took me another fifteen
years to do that. Looking back now I realise that I was
on a downward trend in life that only Jesus could save
me from. I wish I had opened my heart then to Jesus but

I was too caught up in loving myself to even think about loving Jesus.

I settled into the house quite quickly, and grew to love it. It felt good to know that at last I had given Yvonne a house she could call her own. The neighbours were a lovely bunch of people who went out of their way to make us feel welcome, and before long we were all popping into one another's houses without even knocking. Harewood Road was very similar in atmosphere to Coronation Street.

From the time we moved into Harewood Road our career seemed to move into top gear. Before long we were topping the bills in the big nightclubs and were getting a reputation in show business as a good act. One day our manager phoned to tell us he had got us a spot on a TV programme that was running in those days called *The Wheeltappers' and Shunters' Social Club*. The programme was the brain-child of a man named Johnny Hamp. He was a lovely man who loved variety. It was he who brought us *The Comedians* and many more wonderful shows of that nature. Sadly he no longer works in television, and even sadder there are few men like him left in TV. It is now run by accountants and people who don't know what the general public wants, and those that do usually have their hands tied by greater powers. (Now I've got that off my chest I feel better.) The show was made in the studio and the set was made to look like a working men's club, hence the title *Wheeltappers' and Shunters' Social Club*. The set was so realistic that many viewers thought it was a real club, and people would write in and ask if they could become members.

The show was hosted by Bernard Manning and Colin Crompton, two comedians I have looked up to all my life, two wonderful comics who knew exactly how to work an audience. Bernard was the host and Colin played the concert chairman wearing a flat cap. Bernard is in my opinion Britain's best stand up comedian. Colin sadly is

no longer with us, but when he was he looked as if the
sea of life had washed him up on the beach and left him.
He was also a great comic. They had both learned their
craft in the nightclubs, going great in one place and dying
in the next. They both knew how to please different audi-
ences and it was a pleasure to watch them, unlike most
of the young alternative comics today who think that to
be funny you have to swear or be political. It's a shame
that they have nowhere to hone their talents. (Here I go
again, running away at the mouth, but I thought that
you should know that bit of useless information.)

Tommy and I learned a lot from Bernard and Colin.
Bernard had a cabaret club in Manchester and Tommy
and I used to work there before we became comics, and
Bernard used to give us advice. A lot of people don't know
but he has one of the biggest hearts in show business.
Anyway the night came to do the show and we went down
to the studio. It had been years since we had been in a
TV studio (the *Opportunity Knocks* days) and Tommy and
I felt strange having to do the act in front of cameras.
We were very nervous and Bernard could see it, so he
took us to one side and told us to forget about the cameras
and just work the act as if we were working his club. We
took his advice and went on. We stormed the audience
and were asked to come back again. (Thank you,
Bernard.)

Meanwhile back on the home front Yvonne had taken
control of the money and was paying all our bills and
giving me spending money. I know this doesn't sound
right but it was my idea. But one day I got fed up with
the situation and told Yvonne that as I was the man of
the house I should take control of the money and pay
all the bills. (I can just hear all you feminists screaming
now, but I am sorry, ladies, I am what I am.) Yvonne
agreed, first making me promise that I *would* pay all the
bills. She didn't want to go back to the bad times, she
said, when all we had was debts. I told her not to worry,

that I was not a child any more and that I knew what my priorities were. I took control of the money and, about a week after, I was walking through Shaw when I noticed a tumble drier in a shop window. I knew that Yvonne had always wanted one, so I decided to buy it for her. I went into the shop and told the man that I wanted to buy the tumble drier in the window. He asked if I wanted it on hire purchase. I told him I would be paying cash, and asked if he could tie a big blue ribbon around it. He looked at me as if I had gone mad. I mean, who puts a blue ribbon around a tumble drier? But he did as I asked and before long I was heading home with a tumble drier tied with a blue ribbon. When I arrived home I told Yvonne to go upstairs and not to come down until I shouted. She asked what was wrong and I told her everything was fine, it was just that I had a surprise for her. She went upstairs and I got the tumble drier out of the car and set it down right in the middle of the lounge. I then shouted Yvonne down and waited for her. She came in, saw the tumble drier and let out a scream. I thought something was wrong until I saw the scream was from excitement. I was almost as excited as Yvonne, it was good to see her happy. She seemed to ask me a hundred questions all in one breath.

Where did I get it from?

How did I manage to get it home?

When did I see it?

Eventually she calmed down and just sat there looking at it. After a while she asked me the million-dollar question.

How did I manage to pay for it?

I told her not to worry, but she was adamant. I explained that I had decided to leave the bills this week and would pay double next. I saw a shadow of anxiety cross her eyes. She had let me take control and I had blown it. She sat me down and explained to me that we wouldn't have double the money next week to pay the

bills. Then I knew in my heart that I had let her down
once more. I tried to explain that I had only wanted to
see her happy, and that it wouldn't happen again. She
just smiled at me and said that she understood. That was
the day I realised that money was one of my weaknesses,
and from that day to this Yvonne has always taken care
of our finances.

For two reasons 1976 was a very important year for
me. One of the reasons was because we got an offer to do
a pantomime at the Bradford Alhambra. And the second
and most important reason was that it was during this
pantomime that I met a man who would play a crucial
part in my life. We had been offered the role of the
broker's men in the production of *Jack and the Beanstalk*
starring Charlie Drake and Jack Smethurst. Tommy and
I were very excited about doing the panto because we
had never done one before. And it meant we would be
doing real theatre at last. When we got the scripts we
realised that we would be the fourth comics on the bill
(which means that we would be the last to get any laughs,
because the other comics would have all the laughs before
us). It didn't bother us too much, as we reasoned it was
a chance to learn. When we read the scripts we didn't
understand certain things, like 'enter O.P.' or 'exit U.S.'
or 'stand C.S.'. Because Tommy and I didn't know what
these things meant we decided to ignore them. We soon
found out what they meant, much to our embarrassment.
On the first day we met Charlie Drake, who was a comic
with a touch of genius. I have never seen anybody since
who could make an audience laugh one minute and cry
the next. And then we met the other star of the show,
Jack Smethurst, who was a very popular actor of the day.
With Tommy and me being only the fourth comics on the
bill we were more or less looked on as part of the chorus.
It didn't bother us, as I said before, we were doing real
theatre at last, we had to put make-up on and read
scripts, it was brilliant. After we had met everyone we

started to rehearse the panto. We had learned our lines okay, but it was the other little secret signs we didn't know. We kept coming on in the wrong place, bumping into people as we were going off, standing in the wrong place when we were on stage. We could see the director rolling his eyes at us, and after about half an hour he couldn't have been able to take any more, because he called a halt to the rehearsal. He took us to one side and asked us if we knew what O.P., U.S. and C.S. meant in the script. We lowered our eyes and told him we didn't have a clue. He then told us what these secret abbreviations meant. If it said in the script stand C.S. it meant stand centre stage (simple, isn't it); if it said exit U.S. it meant get off up stage; and enter O.P. meant come on opposite prompt side, that means come on opposite wherever the stage manager was situated. (I know that must have bored you, but I figured that everybody needs a place somewhere in a book that they can turn the light off and go to sleep. Well, that was the place.)

The panto opened and we went down very well. Every night when I wasn't on stage I would be in the wings watching Charlie Drake. It was unbelievable how the audience would go wild as he walked on stage, and then he would stand there for a few moments letting the wave of love from the audience flow over him. I wanted what he had, I wanted to be loved by an audience the way he was. I thought that it would fill this empty feeling deep in my soul that I had been feeling for quite a while. After about two weeks into the panto, I started to go to the discos in Bradford. I was having a great time. By this time I was boozing about four nights a week and enjoying it. I had got a taste for whisky and coke, and this coupled with the ladies was a great ego booster.

One day a man walked into my dressing-room and introduced himself. He told me his name was Max Wigley and that he was the theatre chaplain. I shook hands with him and thought that for the next ten minutes I was

going to be in for a very boring time. I had met God
people before and they always seemed to be holier than
thou, do-gooders. But I was wrong. Max was different
from any God person I had met before. He was only a
young man, but he had a peace about him that I couldn't
understand. His face always seemed to be laughing, but
his eyes cared. He seemed to be interested in anything
one had to say, and he never mentioned God once. We
chatted for a while about how the show was going and
then we said our goodbyes. As he was leaving he asked
if it would be okay if he popped in again. I told him it
would and he left. What I didn't realise was that that
had been my first step on the road to meeting the Lord.

A week or so had passed when there was a knock on
my door. I shouted 'Come in!' and in walked Max. The
Devil must have jumped on my shoulder because I wasn't
glad to see him. Again I thought I was going to have a
boring ten minutes. He sat down and asked me how it
was going, and then he asked me a question that made
me think. He asked me if I was happy. I told him I was
very happy, and he just smiled. At that time I didn't
realise the depth of the question, but he did. For some
reason deep inside me I thought he was attacking me
with that question. I know now that the Devil doesn't
like to be faced with the truth. Because I thought he had
attacked me I retaliated by firing questions back at him.
Thinking back, he had never mentioned the Lord once,
it was I who started to ask questions. But then again
perhaps Max knew I would. I asked him why he wore a
dog collar. Did it make him think he was better than me?
Max just smiled and replied that he didn't particularly
like wearing a dog collar, but that it was one of the rules
of the church that vicars had to wear them. He then
explained that wearing a collar had nothing to do with
loving God, and as far as thinking he was better than
me, he said it was his aim to serve me. He was beginning
to blow my mind away. The way that he was talking

about God was as if he was a personal friend. Now, all my life I had believed in God, but only as a lot of people do, that when I die I wanted to be on the right side. I was sure that as I had done nobody wrong God would look at me and I would be all right. But here was a man telling me that I was all wrong. I tried to explain to him that I hadn't done anything particularly bad and that I had been kind to one or two people along the way, and I also told him that whenever I was in trouble I prayed too. He just sat listening to me trying to make excuses for myself. And it was beginning to unnerve me. So I asked what made him so sure that he would end up in heaven. What he told me took me another twelve years to fully understand. He told me that he had asked the Lord to forgive him for being a sinner, and that the Lord had entered his life. I didn't fully understand what he meant by this, because at that stage in my life, like most people, I didn't class myself as a sinner. I didn't understand that from the minute I was born I was a sinner. We talked for about half an hour, discussing the Lord and various things, and then I made my excuses and went on stage.

A few days later he called again. I was beginning to feel that I could never get away from him. We talked for a while and then he said he had brought me some books to read. I felt guilty that I was feeling so resentful towards him. When we had finished talking he asked what we were doing after the show. I told him I was going to a disco and that I was ready for a good night. Suddenly he asked if it would be possible to come with us. I almost laughed.

'No!' I told him. 'I'm not going out with somebody wearing a dog collar, and besides, you might stop me pulling women if they know I'm with a vicar.'

He looked at me and laughed.

'No problem,' he said, and he took his dog collar off. 'See! I'm just like you now.'

I laughed and invited him along. We had a great night, and he became a wonderful friend. At the end of the pantomime run we said farewell to one another and went our separate ways, he with his God and me with my career. It was to be over twelve years before I would be the one who was knocking on Max's door. And on that occasion he would lead me to find God for myself.

6

The fame years

Let us move on a couple of years. By this time Tommy and I were topping bills in small clubs and had worked our way up in theatres to second top. I remember the first time we topped the bill in a nightclub. It was at the Fiesta Club in Sheffield, and we had been there many a time as a support act. And that particular week Matt Munro was topping the bill and as the week started on a Sunday we turned up as we usually did for band call in the afternoon. When we got there we were told by the manager that Matt Munro had had to cancel because he was not feeling well. Now, the manager liked Tommy and me so he told us he was going to put us top of the bill. Tommy and I couldn't believe what he was saying. This was a big nightclub that seated about twelve hundred people and he was giving us a chance to top the bill. We felt half nervous and half excited, and a little bit unbelieving. The manager could see by our faces that we didn't believe him so he took us outside to where the billboard with the stars' names in lights was situated. We watched as a man pulled Matt Munro's name down and put ours up. It was a wonderful feeling to see for the first time our name up in lights, 'Starring all week, Cannon and Ball!' We went back into the club and the manager put us in the stars' dressing-room. Tommy and I were amazed. It had a shower, settees and a bar full of every conceivable drink one could think of. The beauty of it was that the star didn't have to pay for what he drank. So, as the manager said, 'we were the stars'. I felt a million dollars.

We settled in and waited for the first night to arrive and arrive it did. We went round all the other dressing-rooms saying hello to all the other 'supports'. As we were saying our hellos one of the other acts pointed out that we were in for a rough night. We couldn't understand this so we asked them why. They told us that all the audience had booked to see Matt Munro and they wouldn't be getting what they'd paid to see. We could see that they were right and this put untold pressure on us. We went back to the dressing-room and started to panic. What if they didn't like us? What if they booed us off? What if they all walked out? Tommy and I talked about all these questions, and the more we talked the more nervous we became.

Before we knew where we were it was 'top of the bill time'. Us! The compere explained to the audience that Matt Munro was unable to make it and then he introduced us. We went on and the place was packed. Five minutes into our act we had them eating out of our hands. We had a fantastic night, we couldn't have gone down any better. We came off and the manager was in the wings waiting to shake our hands. He told us that we had no problem, we could top the bill all week. We felt like stars. We stayed on at the club basking in our glory. I was in no hurry to rush home to Yvonne, this was far more exciting.

The following night we went to the club ready to slay them again. But when we got there the manager was waiting for us. I knew something was wrong by the look on his face. He told us that the club owners had been in touch with him and they had got Freddy Starr to top the bill for the rest of the week. He apologised, saying that we were still on the bill. Then he dropped the bombshell. With Freddy and ourselves both being comedians, we would have to go on before the girl singer so that we didn't clash. Not only had we dropped from top of the bill, now we were at the bottom. The manager kept apologising but nothing he said could lift the dejection we were feeling. We looked up and saw that our names were already down and Freddy Starr's name was in our place. We made our way sadly to the stars' dressing-room and emptied it of our clothes. We looked around at the free booze and the showers and made our way to our little supports' dressing-room along the corridor.

After we had been on I stayed around to watch Freddy. I could see why he was the top of the bill. He was and still is a comic genius. I watched him and realised that I had a long way to go to be anywhere near as good as he was. Even today I am his number one fan. I think he is the most underrated comic this country has. By the time the week had ended Freddy and I had become close friends, and even to this day I still count him as a friend.

Time went on and we started to earn good money so Yvonne and I didn't have to worry too much. We even decided to move house to a better one we had spotted that overlooked a golf course. We put ours up for sale and before long we had sold it and moved into our new house. It was an old prewar semi-detached with lots of steps leading up to the front door. It was a lovely old house with lots of character. The only drawback was the golf course. The first tee was right at the back of my garden, and I can tell you if there is one thing I don't like it is golfers who think it is something special to hit a little white ball and then go and walk after it. Allow me to explain! One day I was playing with Joanne outside in the garden and she was running around shouting and giggling. Suddenly a man who was on the first tee shouted to me in a voice that sounded like he was chewing marbles (try talking while you are chewing a marble and you will be surprised how posh you talk).

'Excuse me,' he shouted, 'would you mind keeping that child quiet, I am trying to tee off.'

I looked at him and all I could see was a pompous old man. I could feel my temper rising.

'I will not keep the child quiet,' I shouted back. 'And another thing, this is private property and if my child wants to scream and shout it is her prerogative to do so.'

He looked back at me, not knowing what to say, but I had him on the run and I wasn't about to let go.

'And something else you had better think about,' I continued, 'you had better be quiet in future when you are teeing off, because if I hear you shout "FORE!", I will have you for disturbing the peace.'

He quickly hit his ball and he was off. And from that day the golf club and I never saw eye to eye.

I remember quite vividly the start of my fame years, my adulation years, my money years, whatever you wish to call them. I call them my shallow years, because since I became a Christian I realise now that no matter what anyone attains in this world it is shallow without God. But more about that later.

In 1978 Tommy and I were doing a club called the Heart of the Midlands in Nottingham and our manager Laurie Mansfield (by this time we had two managers, one in the north and Laurie in London) sent a man named Peter Woodley from his office to see us in the Midlands with a producer from London Weekend Television. Peter Woodley was one hundred per cent behind Tommy and me. He used to come to a lot of our gigs and told us that it was his life's goal to get us to the top. We believed him, and it felt good to have somebody who believed in us that strongly. He had previously brought everybody and anybody from television to see us but they had always knocked him back saying that we weren't right for television. But Laurie Mansfield, Stuart Littlewood and

Peter had faith in us, so at least we had three people rooting for us.

Peter phoned us up in the afternoon and told us that the producer was making excuses not to come, but he would try his best to get him there. So by the time it got to ten thirty that night we thought they weren't going to make it. We went on stage and paralysed them. The crowd went crazy, they were up on their feet shouting 'Encore, encore'. We took four bows that night. We came off wishing that the man from London Weekend had been there to see it. Just then the dressing-room door opened and in walked Peter Woodley with the television producer. Peter told us that they had just made it in time to see our show. He then introduced us to the producer. He said his name was Humphrey Barclay and that he had enjoyed the show. He was a nice man who seemed very interested in our act. He asked us lots of questions and then he left saying that we would meet again. Peter told us later that on the train back to London he spent half an hour trying to sell us to Humphrey, and all the time Humphrey was saying to him that he liked us. But Peter kept on selling us. Eventually Humphrey stopped him mid-sentence and said, 'Peter, will you stop trying to sell me the act. I have been trying to tell you for the last half hour that I like them.'

Peter then realised that he had been so used to people putting us down that when somebody said he liked us he couldn't believe it. We heard nothing for a while and then Laurie Mansfield called us and told us that London Weekend Television was doing a programme called *Bruce's Big Night Out* starring Bruce Forsyth. He went on to say that the programme would last three hours and it would consist of lots of different things, and that Humphrey Barclay, the producer who had seen us in Nottingham, had wanted us to do six five-minute segments to fit within the show. We were over the moon. At last, a chance to make it big.

That summer we were in Great Yarmouth with Larry Grayson (famous for his catch-phrase 'Shut that door'). We were there for twelve weeks and the television company wanted us to record the segments during the summer. This created problems for us as we had already signed the contracts for the season. We realised that it was too good an opportunity to miss so we asked the promoter who had put the season on if we could have some Fridays off to record the television show. Thankfully he said yes. It was going to be a long slog for Tommy and me, because it meant that every day for six weeks we would have to travel to London to rehearse and then back to Great Yarmouth for the show at night.

We met the writer, a man called David McKellen, and instantly got on with him. He had written us six five-minute sketches. They were very funny, but neither Tommy nor I had done a sketch before. They needed acting out and Tommy and I had never acted before, we were just two comics. Nevertheless we learned the lines and hoped for the best. Summer came and we made our way up to Great Yarmouth. It was great, we settled into the houses we had rented for the summer and then went out on the town to enjoy ourselves before the hard work started. The show soon got under way and Tommy and I were going down quite well. The day arrived for us to go to London to rehearse the sketches, so the night before Tommy had suggested that we went to bed early because we had to catch the six o'clock train the following morning to London. I couldn't go to bed because when I came offstage my adrenalin was still pumping around my body and it took me quite a long time to come down. So Tommy went home to bed and I went off to the nightclubs. I must have had a lot to drink because no sooner had my head touched the pillow than it seemed I was on the train heading towards London and fame. I can still feel my head bouncing off the train window as I kept dropping off to sleep.

We arrived in London and headed for the rehearsal room. When we arrived we met the man who would be directing us. His name was Geoff Sax, and he was a lovely man who helped us tremendously in those early days. He seemed to sense that Tommy and I were out of our depth so he went out of his way to make us feel at home. We rehearsed the first day and soon got into the swing of things. Before long it was four o'clock and time to catch our train back for the show. We caught the train full of excitement and expectations for the future, and arrived in Great Yarmouth with just enough time left to get to the theatre before we were on. We did this every day for six weeks: up every morning for the six o'clock train to London; rehearse the sketch and then back on the train to Great Yarmouth for the show.

Friday was the night that we recorded the show, but during the day we had to do a camera rehearsal. This was very tiring because all day one just went over and over the sketch so that the cameras knew exactly where the moves were and so on and so on. During the afternoon of the first recording Humphrey came into the studio and called me to one side. He asked me why I parted my hair down the centre. I told him that I had always done that because it made me look funny. He looked at me for a moment and then gave me the best advice anyone has ever given me. He told me that I was naturally funny and what I was doing was called gilding the lily. I didn't understand what he meant, and I didn't want to look foolish so I just nodded my head. He could see that I didn't understand so he told me that to be truly funny comes from a comic's inside and not his appearance. Now I understood. All these years I had been parting my hair down the middle so that people would think, 'Ah, here comes a funny man,' instead of them finding out for themselves. I thanked him and 'un-parted' my hair. And if he hadn't given me that advice today I might have been a different Bobby Ball. We went on in the evening and recorded the sketch. It went down very well considering that Tommy and I had never acted before.

After about two weeks of this heavy schedule I was getting fed up with getting up early, the train journey and then going to bed early. I told Tommy I was having no fun, that I wasn't having a proper drink, not to mention all the women I was missing. He told me that I would have to hang in there because this was a chance of a lifetime and we couldn't afford to mess it up through my wanting to enjoy myself. I agreed, but I wasn't going to listen to him. That night after we had finished the show Tommy and I said our goodbyes, he heading for home and me for the nearest disco. I boogied nearly all night, getting back to my rented house about four o'clock in the morning feeling the worse for the booze. I set my alarm clock for five thirty and then fell on the bed in a drunken stupor. Suddenly my eyes shot open and I knew something was wrong, I looked at the alarm clock and it said six o'clock. I had overslept, not only that, I was still wearing the clothes I had been out in the night before. I quickly changed my clothes and set off for the station like a man whose bottom was on fire. When I got there Tommy was waiting, he wasn't at all happy. He told me, tapping his foot, trying to control his temper, that we had missed the train. The next one was at eight o'clock, and to make matters worse it wasn't an express train. I was feeling very guilty so I apologised. I was beginning to feel like a little boy at school. He calmed down and said we would catch the eight o'clock train and take our chance. Eventually the train came and we got on. Tommy wasn't speaking to me. Mind you, he didn't have a chance because I kept apologising. When we got to London we got in a cab and told the driver to hurry as we were now four hours late. When we reached the rehearsal room there was nobody there. It was empty! On a table in the centre of the room was a note. Tommy picked it up and read it out. It said that they had got sick of waiting and had gone back to the studios; we had broken our contract so they had no alternative but to terminate it.

Tommy and I looked at one another, I could tell that he was feeling as I was, sick to the stomach. At that precise moment words couldn't express how I felt. If it hadn't been for me wanting to have a drink and show off in front of women, we would have caught the train and everything would have been all right. I looked at Tommy and once again apologised, only this time I meant it. It was my fault and not Tommy's that this had happened. He just looked at me and told me not to worry, we would have to try again. Suddenly from behind tables and out of doors jumped Geoff Sax and all the television team. They were laughing their heads off. We realised then that we had been set up and they had played a prank on us. I can't tell you how relieved we were. We tried to explain why we were late but they wouldn't listen, they just kept going on about how they had wound us up. Tommy and I looked at one another and knew that we had been lucky. Anybody else apart from Geoff Sax would have sacked us. With a sense of relief and gratitude we spent what little time we had left rehearsing.

We spent the rest of the season rehearsing and recording the shows and then we sat back to wait for them to be shown. They showed the first programme of the Bruce Forsyth *Night Out* and it was a disaster. I thought Bruce was brilliant in it, but the format was wrong. But an even bigger disaster was that we weren't on it. We phoned Laurie Mansfield in London and he told us that the programme was too long and that the heads of London Weekend had decided to scrap the segments that we had recorded. We were devastated. All that work for nothing. It wasn't as if we were paid a fortune for it. We got £400 a show. He told us not to worry, at least we were working.

It's funny but sometimes acts think that managers don't do anything besides sit in an office and draw money. (Don't think that I am praising managers and agents,

I'm not, because a lot of them are sharks who are just in
this business to rip acts off.) But there are a few who
work hard for their acts. This type of manager doesn't
tell the act what they are doing in case the act gets disappointed. That's what happened with Laurie Mansfield.
When he told us not to worry we thought he wasn't
bothered, but he was. He went along to London Weekend
to see one of the top men there at the time, a man called
David Bell, who sadly passed away not long ago. He is
missed in television because he loved variety and was
responsible for a lot of the good television that we saw
in the early eighties.

Laurie told David that he wasn't happy with them not
showing Cannon and Ball and that he wanted to see the
man at the very top. David said he would arrange an
appointment for him and he would go along too, as he
was a fan of ours. The next day Laurie and David went
along to see the man who ran London Weekend Television. His name was Michael Grade and he was a very
powerful man. He asked Laurie and David into his office
and invited them to sit down. Laurie refused, saying he
preferred to stand. He then asked Mr Grade why he was
not showing us. Mr Grade told Laurie that it was nothing
to do with us personally, it was just that the idea of a
three-hour show wasn't working, he had to cut a lot of
things out and we happened to be one of those things.
Laurie then told him that he didn't think it was fair as
we were human beings and not a product. He then went
on to tell him just how hard we had worked, travelling
from Yarmouth to London every day and so on and so
on. Mr Grade said he understood and felt sorry for us,
but there was nothing he could do, he had a television
station to run. Laurie then asked him if he had seen any
of the stuff we had recorded. Mr Grade said he hadn't, so
Laurie asked if he would take a look at it. He replied
that he would at his first convenient moment, and Laurie
and David left his office.

He didn't tell us any of this and I only found that story out when I started to research this book. Mr Grade was true to his word because that same night he watched a video of what we had recorded. The next morning he phoned Laurie at his office and told him that London Weekend were prepared to give us our own series. This was brilliant news, at last we were going to be stars. For me it was also the start of the road which would eventually lead me to find God.

It all seemed to happen rather quickly. One minute we were bottom of the bill and now people were ringing our managers wanting us to top. We were told that we had to go to London for a few days, first to meet David Bell and secondly to meet the writer who was going to write our series. We arrived in London with instructions to meet David Bell at two thirty at the Ritz Hotel for afternoon tea. To think about it was unbelievable; there were Tommy and I, two red-nosed comics from council estates in Oldham, meeting one of the most important men in show business in the Ritz Hotel for afternoon tea. I had never been to a meeting before, so I asked Yvonne if I should go dressed-up or casual. She told me to go how I personally felt comfortable. She had no need to tell me twice. I put on my jeans and a tee shirt, and an old duffel coat that had become a second skin to me and set off for the meeting.

When Tommy and I arrived at the Ritz, the maître d' looked at me horrified. I don't think he had ever had anyone in jeans and a tee shirt arrive at his establishment before. He quickly took me to one side and explained that he couldn't allow anyone in without a tie. Luckily David Bell spotted us in trouble and explained to the maître d' that we were guests of his. The maître d' spluttered and coughed for a while trying to show his authority then finally backed down, saying that he would find me a tie from somewhere. I felt like a second-class citizen, all because I hadn't got a tie on. After I had put my borrowed tie on (which looked more stupid than if I hadn't worn one, because I was wearing a tee shirt which had no collar, so the tie was sitting on my bare neck) we sat down in the lounge and made light conversation, while David signalled for the maître d'. He came over and took our order for tea and sandwiches. After he had gone we started to discuss the series. Before long he was back again asking if I would like to take my duffel coat off. I said yes and handed it to him. The look on his face was a picture. I thought he was going to have a heart attack. He told me that 'sir' would have to wear a jacket. It's funny, isn't it, how some people can call you 'sir' yet look at you as if you had leprosy. Well he was one of those. Not only was he making me feel very small but I felt he was taking away whatever credibility I had with David Bell. I looked at the maître d' and told him that for me to wear a jacket would be an impossibility because I didn't have one with me. He then told 'sir' not to worry, he would get me one. He took my treasured duffel coat away and came back with a jacket, which I subserviently put on.

There I was, sitting in the middle of this cornucopia of affluence in borrowed clothes, feeling about as welcome as a fly on a cow's bottom. I looked sheepishly at David, wishing the ground would swallow me up. But all he did was laugh, he understood the ridiculousness of it all. Before long we were all laughing, and I knew that David was one of us, a person who laughed at all the pomp and hypocrisy that is in the world. Suddenly the 'sir' person was back with our tea and sandwiches, and it took all our strength to keep from laughing. After we had our meeting we prepared to leave and David said he would get the bill. I gave my borrowed clothes back as David was paying the bill. I just couldn't believe the price, it was about £40. It was incomprehensible to me how a few sandwiches and tea could cost that. It was only about £1 for a packet of tea bags and about 54p for a loaf of bread, so how they get away with prices like that I will never know. But then again perhaps I am being too logical.

Our meeting the next day was with the writer. David had told us that they had commissioned a man called Sid Green to write the series. He told us we had to meet him in London Weekend's restaurant. Tommy and I were looking forward to meeting Mr Green, because to us he was and still is a comedy legend. He had written most of Morecambe and Wise's material and now he was going to write for us. It seemed that everything was going right for us. We walked into the restaurant and I saw him seated at a table eating his lunch. David, Tommy and I walked over to where he was sitting and sat down. David introduced us to him and we said our hellos. He just looked at us and then went back to eating his meal. We thought we had done something wrong. I looked at David and he just sat there with a mischievous smile on his lips, he was waiting to see what would happen when three big egos got together.

After an embarrassing silence of about two minutes that seemed an hour, Sid looked up and looked directly at me. He slowly put his knife and fork down and said, 'Well, to tell you the truth, my wife doesn't like you.'

Both Tommy and I were dumbfounded. This was something we most definitely weren't expecting.

'I've watched those things you recorded,' he continued, still looking at me, 'and you have a lot to learn.'

Tommy and I couldn't answer, it was as if we had lost our tongues.

'And another thing,' he said. 'Those silly braces and those stupid Hush Puppies will have to go.'

Now he had said the wrong thing. It was one thing to tell us that his wife didn't like us and that we had a lot to learn, but to tell us that my braces and Hush Puppies would have to go, he had definitely stepped over the line. I wasn't going to have a man sit there and tell me that

the character that I had worked hard to find for the last
fifteen years was going to change overnight. I looked at
him and he had gone back to eating his meal.

'Excuse me, Mr Green,' I said.

'Yes,' he replied, looking up at me.

'My braces and my Hush Puppies will be staying,' I
said. 'And another thing,' I continued, 'as for your wife
not liking us, my wife has never liked Morecambe and
Wise, particularly when you were writing for them.'

I was lying, of course, my wife liked Morecambe and
Wise as much as I did, but I had to get my own back
somehow. He slowly put his knife and fork down and
looked at me. I thought I had ruined our chance of working with one of the best writers in show business, but I
had to say what was in my heart. His face slowly started
to break into a grin and then he laughed.

'I think we can work together,' he said.

What I hadn't realised was that he had said those
things to see how I would react. Obviously I reacted in
the right way, because Sid not only wrote our first series,
but wrote many more after that. It was his material that
made us famous, and I would like to thank him for everything he taught us.

We went back home and then a few months after, we
returned to London to record the series. It was a whole
new ball game for Tommy and me. London Weekend had
booked us into the Savoy Hotel and with limousines to
take us everywhere we were living like stars. It was abso-
lutely mind-blowing. We recorded all the series and
Tommy and I thought they had gone well. Sid was
pleased and to me that mattered more than anything
else. At this stage we were relatively unknown but that
was soon to change. The series was due out and all the
press had got behind us, building us up and saying that
we were going to be stars. Everything was ready for the
big day. But about four days before the series came out
the technicians at London Weekend went on strike. Our

series wasn't going to be shown. It was pandemonium. Laurie Mansfield and David Bell started to have panic meetings. Laurie needed the show to be shown, otherwise all the plans he had made for the future would be jeopardised. The press started to call us Cannon and Blackout, which I thought was very funny. But it must have been a horrendous time for Laurie, because if the strike went on longer than the time we had been allowed for our slot, then we wouldn't get shown until the following year. Luckily for us the strike was called off just in time and our series got shown. The response was something beyond our wildest dreams. Suddenly after years of obscurity everybody seemed to know us, and it was mindblowing. Everywhere we went people would be shouting out our names, in the streets, in the pubs, even taxi drivers in the centre of London would stop their cabs and shout out our names.

'Hello, Bobby, hello, Tommy,' they would shout. It was as if they knew us personally.

It was something that we were not used to, and we liked it very much, it made us feel accepted. When we got half way through our series London Weekend offered us a three-year contract at a fee that had never been paid to anyone before, so our future was looking secure. But Tommy and I never thought about that, we were too caught up in the adulation that we were receiving.

The first season we did topping the bill in a theatre after our first TV series had been out was in 1980. We were booked to do fifteen weeks, two shows a night at the North Pier Theatre, Blackpool. It was quite a daunting thought as we had never topped a bill before. But we had no need to worry. We went to rehearsals and met the other acts on the bill. At the bottom of the bill was a young comic, who I knew was destined to be a star the first time I saw him. I told him so too. He was a young black lad with a vitality that was hard to match and he had talent too. But at that stage in his life it was raw.

He would go on stage and work like a whirlwind for ten minutes and come off leaving the audience screaming for more. His name was Lenny Henry, and even then he was the butt of racist jokes that sometimes hurt him, though he pretended they didn't. Later in life Lenny became one of our brightest stars, and he married a very funny lady by the name of Dawn French. After he got married he suffered more racist slurs. But Lenny rose above it all, and it was my honour to have worked with such a talented man at the start of his career. Later on I read what Lenny and his wife Dawn were going through in the papers and my heart went out to them. If only racists could see that in the Lord's eyes everyone is equal, whether you are black, white or yellow, rich or poor. The Lord loves us all the same.

During the first week of rehearsals for our show in Blackpool, as Tommy and I were walking to the theatre we turned a corner that led to a street facing the theatre, and what we saw made us stop dead in our tracks. They had just put up the posters advertising the show, and there it was, a huge poster, about thirty foot long, with our names blazoned across it, 'The Cannon and Ball Show'. It was a marvellous feeling. At last there we were topping the bill at one of the best theatres in the country. And this time there would be no pulling our names down. Suddenly a bus went past with our photographs spread along the side of it. At last we had arrived. Tommy and I went into the theatre walking on air. We took the same route the next day, just to have a look at the posters again, only this time we were even more shocked. As we turned the corner, there was a queue lining up to buy advance tickets. But what was amazing was that the queue was about three-quarters of a mile long. It started from the ticket box at the north pier and went all along the sea front right up to the central pier. It was a wonderful sight. There they were queueing to see Tommy and me. This was feeding my egotism and all the time it was making me think more about myself than Yvonne and the kids.

On opening night we walked on stage and we couldn't speak for about ten minutes for the crowd cheering and clapping us. I didn't even have to be funny, all I had to do was look at Tommy and the audience would fall about. Among the audience I could see people dressed up as me, with braces on and curly wigs with moustaches. Many people have asked me where my catch-phrase of 'Rock on Tommy' came from. Well, just before we made it, a star who is a big friend of mine, by the name of David Essex, recorded a song called 'Rock on'. One night during the act Tommy was singing and I started to say 'Rock on Tommy', it stuck and before long people started to laugh at it. Don't ask me why, but they did. And on that opening night in Blackpool all the audience were shouting 'Rock on Tommy'. It has stuck with us ever since. You see a catch-phrase cannot be written, they just happen. That year we broke every box office record that the North Pier Theatre has ever held since it opened. And it had been open for at least a hundred years. The success we had was more than the normal success comedians get, it was more as if we were pop stars. We got mobbed everywhere we went. I know it sounds big-headed but it is the truth. And I am only telling you this because I want you to understand why I eventually needed the Lord's forgiveness.

Quite a funny thing happened that season that I don't think has happened often before. We were packing them in every night, and Lord Delfont who owned the theatre decided to take a trip up to Blackpool to find out what all the fuss was about. He came all the way up the pier only to be told he couldn't get in as every seat had been sold. It really tickled his sense of humour that here he was, the owner of the theatre, and he was being refused admission. But he took it all in good part and came back the following night and really enjoyed himself. All over

Blackpool everyone was selling braces with 'Rock on Tommy' printed on them, and it was amazing to see that suddenly young people started to wear them, not just red ones but braces of every colour. Suddenly braces had become fashionable again. We decided to open our own souvenir shop, and it was strange seeing pens and cups and all sorts of things with our names on them. I was like a tourist myself because I even had a mug with my own picture on to drink from (how's that for egotism?).

That year Blackpool asked us if we would be prepared to switch on their illuminations. This is an annual thing in Blackpool, they spend thousands and thousands of pounds on lights and visitors come from all over the world to see them. And for anyone who comes from the north of England, as Tommy and I do, it is one of the biggest honours there is to be asked to switch on the lights. Tommy and I said we would, and when I told my mother that we were switching on the lights, she said, 'Now you are really a star!' We told the committee which was organising the lights that we had a problem as we were working on the pier and we had two shows to do that night. They worked it out and said that we could switch the lights on between shows. They knew it would be impossible for us to walk down the pier so they organised a car to pick us up and give us a police escort down the pier. This was the first time that a car had been on the pier since it opened so once again we were honoured.

On the night of the switch-on we finished the first show and waited for the car to pick us up. It came in due course and we got in. It was an amazing experience because we had to run through a line of policemen to get into the car. The pier was lined six deep either side of the car with people, they were lined all the way down the pier. It was frightening. I know now what a big rock star feels when he is being mobbed. And we were not rock stars, we were just two little comics from Oldham. The people were pushing and shoving, trying to get at us. I did a silly thing and opened the window a little and before I knew what had happened someone had thrust their hand into the car and was trying to rip a chunk out of my hair. It was horrific. The car slowly made its way down the pier and when we arrived in the square where we had to turn the lights on, forty thousand people were waiting for us. It's no wonder our heads got turned. We began to think we could do no wrong, everything was happening too fast. We ascended the podium to switch on the lights. Forty thousand people cheered their approval. We pulled the switch and Blackpool lit up and me along with it.

As my mother said, now I really was a star. All the dreams I had cherished during the early days of working the clubs with Tommy had now come true. I felt I was standing on top of Blackpool Tower itself. The only trouble was that, while my career had reached its peak, my personal life was about to plunge in the opposite direction.

7

Freefall

Now I was a star my life began to change rapidly. I found that doors started to open for me. No longer did I have to wait to see if I could get into a disco, I was given star treatment. I would get someone to phone up a disco and tell them I was coming and they would set a table to one side for me and my friends. Then when I arrived they would surround us with bodyguards. It wasn't long before I was beginning to think this was all natural. I started to drink whisky very heavily. After a while everything you say and do is being controlled by the alcohol that is running around your brain. I also started to notice that it was quite easy to attract women. I thought it was because of my wonderful looks and my overwhelming personality, but what my pride wouldn't allow me to see was that it was nothing to do with looks or personality. It was because I was on television and it made women feel good to be seen with a celebrity. (The truth of the matter is that I am five foot four, with hair like a toilet brush, gappy teeth, and more wrinkles than a map of the London Underground. Only a woman like my Yvonne could love someone like me. And to tell you the truth I am glad that she does.)

So with the drinking and women I was well and truly

on my way down. As my career was on its way up, my personal life had taken a kamikaze dive towards a crash. But luckily for me Jesus would be there to catch me. Along with women and drinking I found that I was getting angry at the least little thing. If I went out to a disco or had taken a little too much to drink I wanted to fight, and it wasn't that I hated those people I picked fights with, it was just that I seemed to enjoy the atmosphere of it all. It was very easy for me to pick fights because I always had bodyguards surrounding me, not like the poor person I decided to pick on. He had no one, so really he was a much more courageous person than I. I was just a coward. But nevertheless this was how my life was beginning to change.

Yvonne and the kids were beginning to take a place further to the back of my mind as I searched for enjoyment. Don't get me wrong, I loved them and I would never do them any wrong, or so I thought, but more and more I was beginning to think about myself.

I finished the summer season in Blackpool with more enemies than friends. The reason I say that is because I found myself not suffering fools gladly. If something was wrong I used to throw a tantrum because (A) I liked everything to be perfect; and (B) I thought that's what stars did. There was no one there to tell me to stop behaving like a prima donna and act like a normal, decent human being. As Yvonne always says, 'A lot of us don't know we are doing wrong until God shows us.'

After the season had ended Tommy and I went down to London to record a Christmas special and during the time I was there I went really wild. I must have hit every club in London. By this time the management had got us a personal assistant, a man by the name of Trevor Davis. His job was to drive us around and literally do anything that we required of him. Now my egotistical world really opened. I ordered him to do all sorts of things, bring me this, bring me that. He had a terrible job, and if he reads this book I would like him to get in touch with me so that I can apologise for the way I treated him.

Stringfellows Nightclub became my favourite haunt when I was in London. But as I was drunk most of the time, my memory of what I did there has become a blur. One night I can remember vividly however. I'd been drinking quite heavily and some lads and myself decided to finish the night off at Stringfellows. Yvonne had just bought me one of those modern raincoats that went down to just above the ankle, and when I wore it I thought that I looked the bee's knees. When you enter Stringfellows there is the restaurant and a bar and then facing you are the stairs that lead down to the disco.

'Come on, lads, let's go down to the disco,' I shouted so that everyone could see and hear me. The lads started to follow me as I made my way to the stairs. By this time the whole club was watching me as I had made enough noise to wake the dead. I got to the top of the stairs when suddenly, much to my dismay, my heel got caught in the hem of my raincoat. Down I went, head over heels down the stairs, and landed up spread-eagled on my back at the bottom. I could hear all the people in the club laughing at me, and as I looked up I could see my friends looking down at me. They just laughed and then they left me. I should have felt embarrassed, but I didn't. You see the alcohol had numbed my brain. I got up, dusted myself down and went into the disco as if nothing had happened. To tell you the truth I felt I had just made a good entrance.

Yvonne and I were now making quite a lot of money so we decided to move house again. I told her I hadn't time to be looking around for a house and to go and find one she liked (thinking back, as I am writing this book, Yvonne never complained about anything, she just accepted me as I was). I carried on with my show business life while Yvonne and our Mavis went house-hunting.

Eventually Yvonne said she had seen a house and asked if I would go with her to see it. I agreed and we went to see this house that was on top of a hill. It was a beautiful house with a breathtaking view, and it was only two minutes away from my mother and father and our Mavis. We said we would have it and after all the paperwork had been completed we moved in.

It's funny, but the house was named Half Way House, and looking back that's exactly where I was in my life, half way to finding Jesus.

Now I felt that I had kept half of my promise to Yvonne. All those years ago when we were living in our Mavis's back bedroom, I promised her that one day she would have a big house and a big car to go with it. I had got her the big house, now all I had to do was to get a big car. That Christmas Tommy and I were appearing in Coventry in a Christmas special. We had sold out for the run so everything was looking good. A few months earlier I had bought myself the car of my dreams, a Corvette Stingray. Yvonne was very unhappy with it, because it was a sports car with only two seats, so our little Joanne had to be scrumped up between the seats. I know Yvonne was right, but I loved my Stingray, it was an animal. Anyway one particular day Tommy and I decided to play our favourite game, which was to dress up in our oldest clothes and then go around the upper-class car show-rooms to see how the salesmen would react. It was funny but the higher up in the car market you went, the more snobbish the salesmen became. And then when they realised who we were they would run around trying to do everything to get us to buy one of their cars. But more often than not Tommy and I would just walk out pretending to be offended. When we got outside we would laugh like two naughty schoolchildren. This particular day Tommy and I decided to drive into Birmingham and go to the Mercedes dealers to play our game. On the way there we passed a garage that had three gold

Rolls-Royces in the window. This was the place. To our surprise the salesmen didn't recognise us but still treated us as if we were human beings. Tommy and I liked this. After about half an hour in the showroom Tommy had fallen in love with one of the Rolls-Royces. Now he got a crazy idea in his head that we should have one each.

'Come on, Bobby,' he said, using his best persuasive technique. 'Let's get one each. We deserve one after all those years of struggling.'

Apart from my dreams in our Mavis's back bedroom I have never been the least bit interested in getting a Rolls-Royce, but slowly Tommy was talking me into it. After a while he succeeded. The salesman said he would take my Stingray in part exchange, and it broke my heart to see him take it away. I said if he could get all the paperwork together for the weekend I'd collect the car then. In the meantime I phoned Yvonne and told her that I had got rid of the Stingray and bought another car. She asked me what I had bought so I thought I would wind her up. I told her I had bought an MG but she didn't know what that was, so I told her it was a little sports car, with wire wheels, and that it was red. I don't think I have ever heard Yvonne shout like she did then. She told me I was a selfish person and that I wasn't being fair to Joanne, because we couldn't go out as a family. I knew how she was feeling but I wasn't going to back down from playing my little joke. I told her that I would be home at the weekend and then she could see it. I also told her that it was the car I had wanted all my life. She put the phone down, saying to me sarcastically that as long as I was happy that was all that mattered. I wanted to give in and tell her I was only joking but I decided to carry on with my joke.

The weekend came and the salesman delivered my Rolls-Royce to the theatre. It was shiny gold with a private number plate. The number plate was JR 17. I didn't know what it meant but it felt good. After the show I set

off for home in my new car. I find it hard to describe the
feeling of driving a Rolls-Royce, some people love them
and some people hate them. Me? I just didn't feel as you
should when you first buy a Rolls-Royce. I just felt that
an ordinary working person like myself didn't belong in
one. Don't ask me why but that's just how I felt. Anyway
I put these feelings to the back of my mind and made my
way home. When I arrived I put the car in the garage as
quietly as I could then went through to the lounge where
Yvonne was sitting.

'It's in the garage, Yvonne,' I said, trying not to laugh.

If looks could kill then I should be dead. She looked at
me as if I had committed a murder.

'I don't want to look at it,' she said. 'I still think that
you are one of the most selfish people I have ever known.'

I begged and cajoled her and eventually she gave in.
We walked in through the kitchen to the garage and
when she saw the Rolls-Royce she let out a scream.

'Where did you get the money from?' she screeched.

I told her not to worry as it wasn't a new car, but a
second-hand one. (Later the press wrote that Tommy and
I had bought two new gold Rolls-Royces, but in fact they
were two second-hand ones costing £17,000 each, roughly
the price of a new Granada.) She calmed down and said
that she was happy, because she had been really worried
that I had bought another sports car.

The next day we went off to show my mother and
father, and to make them really proud of their son. As
we drove there I could tell that Yvonne wasn't enjoying it at all. I asked her what was the matter and she
told me that she didn't like it, she said it made her feel
like a snob. She had put into words exactly what I was
feeling. A Rolls is a great car, but that day I found it
wasn't for me. As we were on our way to my mother's I
could see people looking at me with contempt, and I felt
I had let them down. The Rolls-Royce had separated me
from the ordinary man that I thought I was. I arrived at

my mother and father's and took them outside to see the car.

'Do you like it?' I asked them, hoping they would be proud of me.

'It's a big 'un, isn't it?' exclaimed my mother.

'It'll be a bit heavy on petrol, that will,' my father quickly followed up.

I realised that they didn't even know what it was, and that they were speaking the truth in ignorance.

'Do you know what kind of car it is?' I asked.

They just looked at it and shook their heads. I could see that they didn't have a clue.

'It's a Rolls-Royce,' I said, trying to whip up a bit of enthusiasm.

'Well, it's nice,' replied my mother, trying to please me.

'Aye, you've done well, lad,' my father said.

I knew that my parents were simple folk and that day I found out just how simple they were. They didn't have time for Rolls-Royces and the material things that the world had to offer. They were just happy with their lot, and as long as their children were all right they were happy.

'Well,' I thought to myself, 'at least I have got Yvonne the big car that I had promised her.'

But 'the big car' didn't last long. I had it for about two months and then got rid of it. I bought another sports car instead, but at least this one had two little back seats. One thing that I did find out from that little escapade was that Yvonne also wanted a simple life, it was I who wanted all the trappings of success. Now I realise that no riches on earth can bring you closer to the Lord, only his grace. My father has a nice saying, 'There are no pockets in shrouds.'

Around 1982–3 we were booked into the Dominion Theatre in the West End of London. We were booked for six weeks at two shows a night, and it was the first time we had worked in the West End, so we were quite worried about how the tickets would sell. The box office at the theatre phoned our management about two weeks before we were due to open and told them that we had sold out for the full six weeks. It was marvellous news, not only were we going to have full houses but we had sold out even before we had arrived. They were now selling tickets on the black market at £50. This news only sent my pride and arrogance higher.

By this time I had a personal assistant of my own. I had offered Trevor, our Mavis's husband, the job and he had accepted. I had known Trev since we were kids so it felt good to have a mate with me. We arrived in London and started to paint the town red. At first Trevor was a bit lost as to what to do in the job, but eventually he turned out to be one of the best in the business. He would lift me up when I got down and was always there when I wanted to moan (thanks, Trev). On a Sunday I would go down to Speaker's Corner. It was amazing but before long I had joined the hecklers who would go out of their way to heckle the religious speakers. There I was trying to shout down these men who were speaking about the Lord. But whatever I said, it never threw them, they had conviction. Perhaps it was this that I didn't understand. They would stand there full of the Holy Ghost praising the Lord and I would be shouting out condemning him. But I always came away thinking more about God than when I went.

During my visits to Speaker's Corner I became friendly with a tramp by the name of Smithy. He was an old man who would tramp around the streets of London but always made his way to Speaker's Corner for the Sunday debates. I can still see him now, wearing a long overcoat that had seen better days and trousers that were ripped, and shoes with holes in them. With him being a tramp he obviously didn't take too many baths, so you had to be careful that you didn't get downwind of him. But I

will never forget his eyes, they were alive, they sparkled
as if they were diamonds, always laughing. Whatever
had happened in his life to send him to those depths I
don't know, but he hadn't lost his sense of humour. One
particular Saturday night during our run at the
Dominion, I looked up into the boxes at the side of the
theatre and saw a lot of celebrities who had come to watch
Tommy and me. This put something in my mind. For
some reason I began to think that those boxes were for
privileged people so I decided to change all that. The
following Sunday I went to Speaker's Corner and told
Smithy that I had booked him a box at one of our shows
and invited him along as my guest. He was as pleased
as Punch. The night that he was coming I asked Trev if
he would meet him outside and show him to his box.
About half an hour later Trev was back and said that he
had bought Smithy some champagne and chocolates and
now he was very happy sitting in the box feeling like
royalty. The news about this tramp in the box spread
like wildfire among the cast. Every time anyone went on
stage they couldn't keep their eyes off Smithy's box.
Inside I was having a secret chuckle to myself. I could
imagine that he felt like a king for the night, looking
down on people instead of people looking down on him.
Tommy and I went on stage and at the end of our act I
introduced him. Everybody's eyes in the theatre looked
up towards Smithy's box. And true to form, he stood up
and took a bow. I don't know what the audience thought
of him, but I didn't care. If it is good enough for celebrities
it is good enough for anybody. I will never forget Smithy,
because he really was one of God's children, but didn't
know it.

My visits to Speaker's Corner started to have an effect
on me. Whenever I came away I felt I had been doing
wrong laughing at the religious speakers and it left me
with a restless feeling in my heart. I started to listen to
what they had to say instead of heckling them, and found

that I was getting interested. I bought myself a Bible and tried to understand it but it was useless, it just didn't make sense to me. Nevertheless I carried on, trying somehow to find the truth that the speakers had talked about. But it was no good, I was looking at words instead of into my heart. I started to talk to Buddhists and Jehovah's Witnesses, in fact anybody who could tell me the truth. But every one of their religions left me empty. There was no one who could tell me what I wanted to know. There were always rules involved. As far as the Lord was concerned I asked all the usual questions, how can God allow such suffering in the world, how was the human race started if Adam and Eve had only three children, how do we know there was really a Jesus, these and many more questions. What I didn't realise was that I had to come to Jesus first before I could learn the answers to my questions. In the meantime I would have to continue on my way until I could no longer turn my face away from Jesus.

Between 1979 and 1980 I met Max Wigley the theatre chaplain again and started to ask him questions about God. Slowly our friendship developed and we became good friends. Whenever I was in Bradford Max would come and see me, and I would always turn the questions back to God. So looking back on it, the Lord must already have been stirring in my life.

From 1982 to 1986 it was crazy. Tommy and I were working non-stop and always away from home. We were continually on the road, so the nights got very lonely. But I could always fill myself with whisky and find a woman to help me through. The routine was always the same. We would get into a town, go to the hotel and check in, then to the theatre, do the show, hit a disco till the early hours of the morning, get drunk, maybe have a fight, and back to the hotel to roll into bed. Then the following morning we would get up and travel to the next town, and the same routine would start all over again, without a night off. There were many downers on the road, but we also had quite a few laughs.

I remember Oxford with fond memories. Trev and I had been out to a disco which finished about three o'clock in the morning and we decided to go back to the hotel. We had parked the car in a municipal car park at the other side of town, so Trev suggested that we got a taxi back to the hotel and picked the car up in the morning. But with the alcohol inside me I was having none of this. Trev tried to make me see reason but it was to no avail. We eventually reached the car park and picked the car up. As we came down the ramp the barrier was down, so I told Trev to put some money into the machine. He just looked at me and said it was no use. I argued that he was talking stupid because all he had to do was put some money in and the barrier would go up. He didn't answer but just pointed to a sign on the wall: 'This Garage is not 24 hour parking.' Trev and I started to laugh, but I wasn't going to be beaten. I told him that if I could lift the barrier high enough, perhaps he could just get the car underneath. (At this time I was driving a Camaro sports car, so it was very close to the ground.) Trev agreed so I got out of the car to try and lift the barrier. It started to move, when suddenly it broke and left me holding half of it in my hands. I looked at Trev and we both started to laugh. But our laughter was cut short by the sight of a police car pulling up in front of us. A young policeman got out and looked at me as if I was one of the great train robbers. Suddenly I seemed to sober up in a minute.

'What's going on?' he asked.

I thought that was a stupid question, but I decided against voicing my opinion. I thought I would explain then he would see that I was an innocent party.

'It's like this, officer,' I said, trying to be as jolly as I could. 'We came and tried to get our car out of the garage but we couldn't because the barrier was down, so I tried to lift the barrier, but I didn't break it.'

'Well, you're holding it,' he said smugly.

I looked down and I was still holding half a barrier. I started to stammer and plead my case, but he wasn't listening.

'Come on,' he said, 'I'm taking you both down to the station.'

'What for?' I pleaded. 'It was an accident.'

'Vandalism,' he replied.

I knew then that he was just after me, and nothing I said was going to change his mind. We arrived at the police station and stood in front of the desk.

'Stand behind that white line,' said the young policeman.

Just then an old sergeant turned up and looked at me and winked. The young policeman whispered a few words to him, and then asked Trev to step forward. Before he had a chance I stepped forward and pleaded with the old sergeant that it was all a mistake.

'Get behind the line!' the young policeman shouted at me.

He was beginning to get on my nerves.

'I have sons as old as him,' I thought to myself but nevertheless did what I was told. Trevor stepped forward and the young policeman asked him to empty his pockets. This really frightened me, because Trevor was carrying about £4000, which he carried to pay for hotels and things during the tour. I could see the policeman's eyes light up. I began to worry that they might think we had stolen it. I knew that I had to explain where it came from, so I stepped forward again.

'You don't understand,' I began.

'Get behind the line,' the young policeman shouted again. But this time I wasn't listening to him. I was talking to the old sergeant.

'You see, we always carry that sort of money when we are on tour,' I continued, trying to get Trev and myself off the hook.

'Get behind the line,' the young policeman shouted again.

'No!' I said, 'because you aren't listening to me.'

'Take him down to the cells,' the young policeman said to another policeman standing by.

'Tell 'em nothing,' Trev said as the policeman got hold of my arm.

I couldn't believe what was happening to me. I was being taken down to the cells and Trev had started acting like a major villain. As I was taken away I could hear Trevor shouting after me, 'Tell 'em nothing.' This was crazy, all over a car barrier that I was willing to pay for. By the time I had reached the cells my attitude had changed. I was beginning to feel like Clint Eastwood in the film *Alcatraz*.

'Can you remove your shoelaces, please?' the policeman asked me.

He was a nice man, who knew that what had happened to me was a mistake, but it wasn't his case so he just had to follow orders. I wasn't bothered how nice he was being, I was now in my gangster mode.

'What do you think I am going to do, commit suicide?' I replied, almost feeling my lip curl.

He just smiled, and continued being patient with me.

'Would you like a blanket?' he asked.

How dare he insult me. I had now become harder than Clint Eastwood. I was Sylvester Stallone.

'No, I'll be fine,' I replied.

I walked into the cell and he locked the door behind me. I looked around the room and at the little peep-hole in the door, and felt terribly alone. It was the first time I had been in a cell and it wasn't a nice feeling. After about ten minutes my gangster mode had left me and I sat on this metal bench, shivering. It was no use, I would have to call the nice policeman back. Swallowing my pride I banged on the door. There was no reaction to my banging, so I kept on banging. After a short while the door opened and the nice policeman was standing there once more with a smile on his face, and holding a blanket.

'Do you want the blanket now?' he asked, as if he knew.

'Is it possible?' I asked in my most subservient voice.

'Course it is,' he said.

'Thanks,' I replied and went back to sit on my bench.

He stood there looking at me for a moment, and I could see that he was starting to feel sorry for me.

'Would you like a cup of coffee?' he asked.

Would I? I could have kissed him. He brought me a coffee, and after about ten minutes they came to collect me. At least I was getting out of the cells. They took me to a little room that was empty and told me to sit down. The door was open and across the corridor from me I could see Trevor arguing with a policeman. Suddenly he spotted me and shouted what had become his catch-phrase, 'Tell 'em nothing.' I turned my eyes away, not wanting to get involved. I sat there for about three or four minutes before the young policeman who had arrested us came in. He sat facing me with a load of papers. Then he started to ask me questions. I answered the truth, and kept telling him that it was all a mistake. But he was having none of it, he was determined to get me for vandalism. We were getting nowhere when the old sergeant came walking in. He whispered something into the young policeman's ear, and they both walked out. After a while the young policeman came back looking rather sheepish. He told me that they were going to forget it this time and let me off with a caution, but I would have to pay for the barrier. I knew then that the old sergeant had been talking to him, and telling him that he was pushing it too far. I agreed to pay for the barrier and then they said I could go.

When I got to the front desk Trev was waiting for me. I smiled at him and then turned around to the young policeman who had arrested me and asked him if he was married. He replied that he was, so I invited him and his wife to the show the following night. He was overjoyed and said it would be great. I shook hands with them all and said that I would see the young policeman at the theatre. When we got outside Trev said I must be crazy asking 'that copper' to the show. But Trev didn't know what I had in my mind. I told Trev to arrange for two seats to be available in the front row for 'my new-found friend'.

The next night soon arrived and Tommy and I went on stage. I saw the policeman there with his wife, and now my time for revenge had come. His joy soon turned to embarrassment when I started to rib him. I didn't just do it for a minute or two, but for at least fifteen minutes. I cracked every gag I could about him, and I think if there had been a hole in the floor he would have crawled into it. We came offstage and I knew that he wouldn't be coming backstage to see me, so I sent Trev to try and find him, but he had gone. So somewhere in Oxford there is a policeman wishing he had booked me for vandalism when he had the chance.

During this time money was no object to Tommy and me. It was the top hotels with limousines here and there, and if we had to travel any further than five hundred miles there would have to be a private plane to take us. I had now started to believe this lifestyle I was living. If we were due to go to a theatre, we would check out what the dressing-rooms were like and if they weren't up to scratch we would have new ones built, even though we would only be using them for one season. Extravagance became our middle name. I remember one time very well when we had been booked to do a private show in Brighton. At that time I was staying in a suite in one of the top hotels in London, so we ordered two limousines; we booked two suites costing £350 each at a top hotel in Brighton; we drove down there, used the £350 a night suites as changing rooms, did the show and then drove back to London. So in all we must have used those suites for all of a quarter of an hour. The Lord must have been looking down at me and shaking his head.

The pressure on Tommy and me at this time was intense. We were two ordinary lads who didn't particularly like all the attention and adulation we were receiving. It had changed me drastically. I was now boozing more than ever, and lust had well and truly got hold of me, not to mention the aggression. Yvonne had got used to me flying off the handle, so to her it was an everyday thing. She began to think that that was the way I was. One day I got a little fed up with myself and decided to change my ways. I told everybody that I had found 'the quality of life' and that I would no longer be losing my temper because nothing was worth it. Trev just rolled his eyes, Yvonne shook her head, and our company manager, a man named Tony Hayes, just smiled. (Since 1986 Tony has been a great strength to me and I would count him one of my closest friends. If ever there was a man one could trust with one's life he would be the man.)

The next day after I had made my statement about the quality of life, we were travelling up to Birmingham from London. We were in the middle of a tour and on one of those rare occasions I had decided to take Yvonne. In the car with us were Trevor and Tony Hayes and his wife Anita. We were driving along very nicely on the M1 when my car decided to break down. Normally if anything like that happened I would have gone berserk, but not this time, now I had 'the quality of life'. Everyone looked at me, waiting for me to blow a fuse, and they were quite surprised when nothing happened. Quite calmly I told Trevor to get the AA and then I proceeded to get out of the car, take a table and two folding chairs from the boot and put them on the hard shoulder. Everyone in the car was looking at me as if I had gone mad. I then took out a chess set and put it on the table, sat down in one of the chairs and asked if anybody was interested in a game. I can still see their faces. They just looked at me with their mouths hanging open. It must have been a sight to see a man at a table on the hard shoulder of a motorway, waiting for someone to play him at chess. Eventually Tony said he would play and he sat down opposite me. They still couldn't get over my quality of life. We had been playing for about five minutes, when a huge lorry flew past and blew the table and all the chess pieces into the grass verge. I jumped up and started to scream every swear word I could think of. My quality of life had gone out of the window. I started to shout after the lorry, but by now it was miles away. I turned round and looked at the others, they were all trying not to laugh, but this only made it worse. I got on my hands and knees trying to find the chess pieces and all the time I was muttering under my breath. I had never felt so annoyed in my life. While I was on my hands and knees, Yvonne walked over to me and tapped me on my shoulder. I looked up at her and she said, 'So much for quality of life, eh!'

She was right, my quality of life had lasted all of two hours.

It was during this time that I found myself having a couple of days at home. But I couldn't stay in with my wife, I always had to be out and about showing myself off. The couple of days that I had off landed on a weekend, so I decided to go for a drink on the Sunday dinner-time with a couple of friends at a local wine bar called Nell Racker's (I know it's a strange name, it was supposed to be named after a local ghost). Anyway we arrived at the place and got settled in at the end of the bar. On one side of me stood a huge man who looked as if he could have killed Mike Tyson. He started looking at me so I started to look back, and after we had looked each other up and down we started to talk and he told me that I had taken the mickey out of him a couple of years earlier at a club in Manchester. I tried to smile but my lips were stuck to my teeth, I didn't know whether he was going to hit me or laugh about it. Luckily for me he laughed about it. We started talking and it turned out that we were both fans of rock 'n' roll; the more I talked to him the more I realised that he was a kindred spirit. After a while I had to go to the toilet and when I got in there a man asked me if I knew who I was talking to. I said I didn't, and he went on to tell me that the man was named Jack Thirsk who had a very dubious past and was known locally as a very hard man. He also warned me to be very careful what I said because Jack would take my head off without thinking about it. This perturbed me a little, because (A) I had been getting on famously with him; and (B) I had become very fond of my head. I went back to my place at the bar and Jack Thirsk was still there. We carried on talking and I found him to be a very interesting man. He told me his name and that he had enjoyed my company. We said our goodbyes, promising to meet again, which we did, and after that meeting we became the best of friends. We eventually ended up going everywhere together, and our wives also became friends. (We even bought the club where we had first met. We named it Braces, but that's another story.) Jack Thirsk has been my friend since the early eighties, and I know that we will be friends until the day we die. I could write a book about the stories Jack told me and one day I probably will. He has been a true friend to me and I have told him things that I would tell no one else. Jack Thirsk has a reputation as a hard man, but I know the real Jack Thirsk, and underneath that hard exterior lies a gentle giant. He is a man who would give his last penny to help someone. I would like to thank him for being such a friend.

As I said before, by now money was no object and I would spend my money on anything that took my fancy. Looking back I am amazed at the type of person I had become. I was drinking more than ever and lusting after women as if it was going out of fashion. The Devil had really got hold of me. I remember one time in Torquay I had a little boat which I had named *Smile*. It was a smashing little boat and we had many a good time on it, but after a while it wasn't good enough for me. I had to have something bigger, something that everyone would look at. One morning I saw a big forty foot boat come sailing into the harbour, and I knew I had to have it. It had a 'For Sale' sign on the side, so all I had to do now was talk Yvonne into having it. I told Yvonne I had seen a boat that I had fallen in love with and that I would like to have it. She reasoned with me that we were only in Torquay for ten weeks and after that the boat would be no good to us. I promised her that I would keep the boat for ever, and that I would never ask for another thing. She gave in to my pleading eyes and phoned the people who owned the boat, telling them that we would be coming down to discuss the details with them. We arrived at the dock and when I saw the boat close up I fell even more in love with it. It was a Tremlett boat with a captain's bridge and all the gadgets that anyone could think of. I could see that it didn't interest Yvonne in the least and that she was only doing this for me.

Now I have never been any good at bargaining so I left it to Yvonne, who is quite good at it. She asked the people the price they were asking for the boat, and they told her £40,000. Both Yvonne and I knew that this was out of our price range, but I had to have it at all costs. Yvonne tried to bargain with them to get the price down, but I didn't let her, I just jumped in and said that I had to have the boat at any price. Yvonne just looked at me, she knew there was no way she could bargain now. We said we would think it over and be in contact with them, then we left. When we got off the boat Yvonne told me in no uncertain terms that there was no way we could afford to spend £40,000 on a boat. It was crazy, she said. I told her that I had to have it, after all I was a 'star'. She gave in once again, and the next day we bought the boat. It was so big I had a hard time handling it. It weighed fifteen tons so you can imagine it wasn't easy.

One Saturday night about two weeks after I had bought the boat, I decided that I was going to take it across the Channel to Jersey for the weekend. I knew a man who said he could take it across with me because he knew what to do. That was all I needed to know. I arranged to go the following Saturday after the show. I didn't tell Yvonne until the following Friday so that it would be too late to back out. Saturday came and after the show as usual I had drunk my daily dose of alcohol. In fact I was rather tipsy. It was a very foolish thing, trying to get across the English Channel half drunk. But in those days nobody could tell me anything. I thought I knew it all. We all got on the boat and set off for Jersey. I was on the captain's bridge with this chap who said he knew what to do, and Yvonne was downstairs in the cabin putting Joanne to sleep. It was fine until we left the sight of land and then I started to sober up. I suddenly got a feeling of loneliness. It was a strange feeling and it made me realise just how foolish I had been. But we were too far out now to turn back. I felt we were the smallest thing in the world and that the sea was the biggest. All sorts of things started to go through my mind. What if we hit a log and it ripped the bottom out of the boat? What if the boat overturned, would I have enough strength to save Yvonne and Joanne? (Yvonne can't swim.) These thoughts and many more went through my mind as I steered the boat. Luckily for us the sea was calm that night, but it didn't stop me worrying. All around us I could see lights from other ships, but I knew that if we went down, they wouldn't know about it.

Suddenly to the starboard side of me I could see a red light that I took to be the back end of a boat. I thought I was all right because it appeared to me to have passed us. So I carried on going straight. Suddenly all these lights went on and sirens started to sound. I wondered what on earth was happening. Then I saw from the lights that the other boat was a mile-long tanker, and I was heading right for the centre of him. I was within a hair's breadth of crashing into him. There he was towering over me like Goliath must have done over David. I thought that my days had come to an end. I banged my boat into reverse and turned the wheel. Through God's mercy I found myself just missing the back of him. But now we were caught up in his wake. We were thrown about like a piece of wood caught up in the rapids. It was all over before we knew where we were, but it had been scary while it lasted. We were once again floating on a calm sea. The man who said he knew what to do then told me that the English Channel was one of the busiest waters in the world. I asked him which way we had to head now. It was then that he dropped the bombshell. He said he didn't know, because he had never left the shoreline before. Thanks! We were now in the middle of the English Channel and we hadn't got a clue where to go. Lucky for him that I had sobered up otherwise I might have thrown him overboard. I knew that Jersey was south of England so I looked at my compass and set a course south. After about an hour's sailing I could see the dark outline of land in the distance. I didn't have a clue where we were so I suggested that we anchored and waited until light. We all agreed and Yvonne and I settled down to get some sleep. The time was now about four o'clock in the morning and it would soon be light, so at least we would be able to see what we were doing.

Yvonne and I had been in bed for about two minutes when the boat started to vibrate with a loud noise which was deafening. I jumped out of bed and dashed on to the deck. Right beside my boat was a trawler that had decided to fish there. I had an intense feeling of relief. At last we had somebody near us who knew what they were doing. I shouted out to them and all the crew came to the side of the boat. I asked them where we were and they all started laughing. They had recognised me and this only made it worse. They started ribbing me, but I was too tired to answer back. After a bit of chitchat I asked what was the piece of land I could see in the distance. Dawn was now breaking so the land was even more visible. They told me it was Guernsey and that Jersey was just around the corner. They could see that we were novices so they warned us that Jersey was very dangerous to approach because of rocks and that we had better phone the coastguard to take us in. We thanked them very much for all their help and set off for Jersey. On the way we phoned the coastguard and they came out and took us into Jersey. Well at least we had arrived safely.

We had a nice weekend in Jersey and then on Monday morning we set off back for Torquay. It was raining slightly when we set off from the harbour, but when we got out into the sea we were in the middle of a force six gale. I have never seen waves so big. They towered over the boat, threatening to swamp us any minute. One minute we were on the top of a wave and the next minute we were down in the belly of it. It was frightening. But it never bothered Yvonne. She only thought I was going too fast. What I didn't know was that with the sea so rough, it was throwing everything around in the cabin and Yvonne was blaming me for going too fast. I realised that it was hopeless, so I phoned the coastguard again and they came and picked us up and took us back into the safety of the harbour. We flew back to Torquay and left the boat in Jersey. It wasn't until a couple of days later that I realised just how reckless I had been with my family's lives. If it hadn't been for the grace of God we might not have been here today. I kept the boat until the end of the season and then sold it, at a loss. So I had spent £40,000 on eight weeks' enjoyment. I am not telling you this to show how much money we had, I am telling you this to show you that I had all my priorities wrong.

And it is only when one finds Jesus that one realises that money, drink, women, even life itself don't mean anything without the wisdom of God.

It was during this time, between 1982 and 1986, that I was full of self-praise and excess, everything I did was to excess. I had everything and yet I had nothing. Slowly I began to feel empty inside. It was okay at first because I didn't notice it. I was too caught up in this fast pace of life. Along with the emptiness came guilt. Guilt at the way I had treated my wife over the years. I tried to put these feelings to the back of my mind by buying some big car or some other material thing that I could get excited about, and it worked for a couple of days and then the feelings would be back gnawing at my conscience. Eventually these feelings tormented me constantly. But I couldn't stop what I was doing. I needed help and it was a lot nearer at hand than I thought.

8

Journey into new life

During 1980 a company called Wigwam were working for Tommy and me. They were a company that did our sound at all our gigs. I didn't realise it at first but later on found out that they were 'Christians'. Not only that but they were 'born-again Christians'. I had read my Bible so I thought I was quite knowledgeable, but I didn't know what a 'born-again Christian' was. Now I know that one can't be a Christian unless one is born again, but it took the Lord to teach me that. Anyway I digress. Two of the men who worked the sound, Mike Spratt and Ken Woodward, were very strong Christians who helped me later on in my Christian journey. It was Mike Spratt who, along with his minister friend Mike Hook and a lot of help from the Lord, started off Wigwam Sound, and now it is one of the largest sound companies in Britain. Later on Mike Spratt was to play a major part in Yvonne's life.

After telling you that, let's get back to me! Having these Christians around me gave me a chance to study them. I had never been this close to one before (apart from Max Wigley, but he was a vicar so in my mind it was his job), but these were ordinary lads in ordinary jobs. They seemed to have a peace that eluded me, but I

thought that I had it right and not them. Even when I
would scream and shout at them they would just smile
back at me. They would never lose their tempers, and they
always seemed happy. Tommy and I were quite pleased
to employ them as our sound crew, but I kept my distance,
I didn't want to become like those 'born-again Christians',
to me they never seemed to have any fun. After the gigs
they would pack up the sound system and then go
straight back to the hotel. That wasn't for me! I was too
busy enjoying my life (or so I thought). Anyway they
didn't have what I had, I had fun, drinking, fighting and
women. But in truth, they had much more than me, they
had learned the truth! And it gave them peace of mind.

Slowly I began to hate the life I was living. I began to
hate the drinking every night, and the things that it led
to, but I couldn't stop, I was too far down the road. I
tried reading the Bible. Why? I don't know, perhaps I
was trying to find God then, but it was no use, even that
didn't bring me any solace. I began to get feelings of guilt,
but as usual I managed to shove them to the back of my
mind. Yet somewhere deep inside me I knew that I had
to face God. But then again, I reasoned to myself, I was
no different from any other man, apart from those 'born-
again Christians'. I hadn't really done anything wrong,
and I was quite sure that God would forgive me when I
was dead. How foolish!

During the Christmas of 1986 we returned once again
to Bradford and as usual my old friend Max Wigley came
in to see me. It was great to see him, now we could have
more discussions and arguments about the Christian
message. I asked him many questions and he answered
them very simply. In fact what he told me made me
realise that God could be very real. What you must
realise was that to me God was only a force, something
found in the Bible and at church or Sunday school. God
was for people who didn't have anything else in their life.
I told Max that now my daughter was growing up I was

becoming very embarrassed about watching a video with her even though it was PG rated, because of the bad language. And I also told him about my concern for the state of the world and how I thought that if Jesus was real he was the only one who could sort it out. Max told me later that he could see Jesus already working in my life, but at that time becoming a born-again Christian was the furthest thing from my mind. Max and I had quite a few talks, and the more we talked the more my guilt came to the surface. A few days later Max came to see me again and said that he felt we should have a talk. It was about an hour before the curtain went up, so we sat down to talk. What he told me changed my life for ever. He told me about the love and justice of God, using this illustration.

One day a judge came into court wearing his fine robes and wig and sat in his elevated chair behind his big bench. He looked into the dock, and there in the dock was his son, whom he loved very much and wanted to forgive for all the sins he had committed. However, as a judge he had to be just and needed to hear the case against his son. He listened as his son's sins were read out. Then after the hearing he pronounced his son guilty, and fined him £500. He then took his wig off and his fine robes and came down from his big chair and bench and walked across the floor of the court. He took his cheque book out, signed a cheque for £500 and paid the fine for his son.

Max pointed out that the judge had been both loving and just and that is what God has done for us through Jesus Christ. I realised that Max was telling me that God knows we have broken his laws and that we deserved to be punished, but he also loves us enough to come himself and take the punishment that we deserve.

This illustration had a great effect on me, I had never looked at God in this way. It made him seem more real. I knew that I needed to be forgiven for what I had done and coming before God as the judge's son had in the illustration seemed the only way. I told Max that I would like to become a Christian that night and asked him if he would wait until the end of the show. He said he would and then went around the other dressing-rooms to see the other artistes. The curtain went up and everyone got on with the show. But as I was going through the show I couldn't get Max out of my mind. Had I said the right thing? Did I want to become a Christian? Was I ready to become one? I felt that I had done the wrong thing by saying I wanted to become a Christian, because I felt I wasn't good enough, I felt I had sinned too much. I also felt that if I committed myself to the Lord and he was real I was sure that I would let him down. It's not that I didn't want to get to know the Lord, it's just that my way of life had become like a drug to me. I felt very frightened and threatened. I realise now it was the Devil that was making me feel threatened, because I was about to walk into the Lord's presence and he would lose a good disciple.

After the curtain came down I went to my dressing-room fully expecting Max to be there, but luckily for me he wasn't. He was in some other dressing-room talking to another member of the cast. I was preparing some lie or other to tell him so that I could get out of this situation when he walked in. I have never felt so frightened in my life. Max told me later that I was deathly white and looked visibly shaken. I felt I was in the presence of God, the room became filled with a peace. I now know that the Holy Spirit was following Max around like an old friend. I knew in my heart that I couldn't face God because I felt too ashamed, so I asked Max if we could leave things that night and told him that I would come over to the vicarage one day when we didn't have a matinee. He said that was okay and just smiled at me. He knew that God was working in my life and it was only a matter of time before I gave my heart to him.

I went home that night a very troubled man. I knew that I had to face the Lord but it seemed such a big step, as if I was about to jump over the edge of the Grand Canyon into the unknown. I felt so frightened. I didn't want to become a monk or a holier than thou. I just wanted to stay me! Only without the sinning. But most of all I wanted to be forgiven. I wrestled with my conscience for a few days, with the Devil trying to cling on to me, but in the back of my mind I knew inevitably what would happen. I didn't tell Yvonne any of this, even though I had spoken about God and the Bible to her many times in the past; this was something just between the Lord and me. I kept on wrestling with my conscience, trying to put God to the back of my mind. But it was no use, I knew that I had to contact Max and talk to him at length about it.

A few days later I telephoned Max and told him I would like to come over and see him. He told me that it would be no problem, and we arranged for me to visit him at his vicarage the following day, Thursday. I told Trevor that he would have to run me over to Bradford where Max was living. Trevor didn't ask why, but just said okay. I think he was used to my crazy schemes by now. I then told Yvonne that I was going to see Max the following day. She asked why and I told her that I wanted to see him, and that I was very interested in God. If only she had known that inside I was frightened in case I actually got to meet him.

Thursday morning came and Trev and I set off for Bradford to see Max. I was very quiet on the journey, which is not at all like me. Trevor must have been wondering what was wrong. What he didn't know was that I felt I was stepping into something that was beyond my control. I didn't know what was going to happen, but I knew that I would be talking about God as I had never talked about him before. We arrived at Max's house and Trevor took me to the door. He didn't wait with me, he was off like a rocket. Max came to the door and asked me in. I was beginning to feel very strange. I thought, I was happy in my old ways, why am I doing this? We went through into Max's study and he asked if I wanted a cup of tea. I would have sooner been out of there but for some reason I stayed. Max and I talked a little about nothing and then we started to talk about God. He then produced a little book called *Journey into Life*. He asked if I would like him to read it to me and I said yes. Do you know, I can't even remember what the book was about, but all I know is after Max had finished reading it, I knew I had to give my life to the Lord. Sorry, I will rephrase that. I wanted to give my life to the Lord. I turned to Max and told him that I wanted to become a Christian, and without any prompting from him, I was on my knees, something I hadn't done since I was a child. At the end of the booklet there is a little prayer and Max asked me if I would like to say it. I told him I would and began to say the prayer. I only got about half way through it and couldn't say any more. Tears began to fill my eyes and I started to cry like a baby. I knew at that moment that the Lord was real, as real as you or me. And not only that, I knew that in his mercy he had forgiven me. I felt clean and alive for the first time in my life, I got a wonderful feeling of exhilaration, a feeling of belonging to God. I felt special. Nothing else mattered to me, only being with the Lord. Through my tears I asked Max to finish the prayer for me. I didn't listen to the rest of the prayer, I was too busy thanking the Lord for saving me. I can't begin to tell you all that I felt, but when God puts his hand on you and loves you there is no feeling like it in this world. I knew that my life had changed and that I was at the start of a new journey.

I know that a lot of people say it's a load of rubbish, and I was one of them, but I'm here to tell you today that finding the Lord is the only way to live, it is impossible without him. People have said to me that when people go to a gospel church and become born-again Christians it is only because of the atmosphere and the minister whipping them into an emotional frenzy, but I found the Lord in a little room of a vicarage, with just another person and me quietly talking about Jesus Christ. So it doesn't matter where you are, if you really want the Lord to come into your life, he will. It doesn't matter who you are, you just have to ask! He is such a gracious Lord that he won't come into your life unless you ask him in.

I thanked Max for helping me to find the Lord and bade him goodbye. When I got to the car Trevor was waiting. I got in and told him that I had found the Lord. He looked at me strangely for a moment and said, 'I'm happy for you but don't try and push it on me.' It made me laugh, suddenly I had become an alien, but do you know, it felt good. All the way home I never spoke, I just wanted to stay within this new-found peace that the Lord had given me. All my questions about God over the years he was now answering very clearly. I was walking on air. It was the biggest high I have ever had, bigger than when we topped the bill at the Opera House, Blackpool for ten weeks to 360,000 people, bigger than when we were the subjects of the TV programme *This is Your Life*, bigger than when we met the Queen. This was bigger than anything that had ever happened to me. I knew God personally, and everything pales into insignificance after that.

I eventually arrived home and broke the news to Yvonne that I had found God and become a born-again Christian. As I was telling her I started to cry again because I was so happy, I was weeping tears of joy. She looked at me a little strangely, and said she was happy for me, but she told me later that she thought it was a fad and sooner or later I would get over it. I'm sure a lot of people thought that, but I am here to tell them that since that time in 1986 I am still the same, 'a lover of God'. I now had a peace about me that I am quite sure must have seemed quite strange to Yvonne and other people, but then again they didn't know the power of the Holy Spirit. As soon as I had finished telling Yvonne about my meeting with the Lord, I looked at her and she seemed different. For the first time in many years I really looked at my wife, and for the first time I was looking at her with Christian eyes. I could now see inside her, gentleness and kindness, and how much she had loved me all these years. I felt so much love for her that it seemed to overwhelm me. Because through God's grace he had taken away my selfishness and replaced it with love for my fellow man; Yvonne is more than my fellow man to me, so you can imagine the love that I was feeling for her. God had given me a true marriage.

For the next few weeks I did nothing but talk about God and how wonderful he was, he seemed to fill my every waking hour. Yvonne must have thought she was living with a different man, because I never lost my temper and didn't swear, I was at total peace within myself. If I think about it, she *was* living with a different man, I was a man who knew the truth about life. And the truth is, one cannot have a life without God. I told my family and friends about being saved and they accepted it without any qualms. A few of my friends took the mickey out of me, but it didn't bother me to any extent because, after what happened to Jesus, a few people taking the mickey out of you seems very trivial. After a few weeks of living with this different man, Yvonne said that she wanted what I had got. I was over the moon, now I thought that Yvonne and I would both be together in God's arms. I phoned Max Wigley and told him that Yvonne wanted to come to the Lord. He asked me if I was sure, and I told him I was, my enthusiasm knew no bounds. I didn't understand then that it is the heart which must want the Lord and not just the brain. I now know that he goes right to the source of our true feelings, the heart.

Max dutifully arrived later that afternoon and we all

got on our knees to pray to the Lord. After we had finished praying I looked at Yvonne hoping to see the Lord within her, but she was no different from before. She told me later that she didn't feel any different, and that she thought that is how Christians should feel. But to me, having had such a revelation of God, it seemed impossible that anyone could just sit there and say that now they were a Christian, without showing any emotion. I asked Max if he thought Yvonne had found the Lord, but he just replied that the Lord works in many different ways with different individuals. We thanked Max for coming over and bade him farewell. Then I started to watch Yvonne for tell-tale signs of her having been saved. But I was in for a big disappointment, Yvonne hadn't changed in any way. What I didn't know was that God was already working in her life and it was just a matter of time. I now realise that when Yvonne, Max and I prayed together, Yvonne was praying only with her mind, but the time was drawing near when Yvonne would pray with her heart and then the Lord would be able to change her life and give her all the wonderful gifts that he has promised everyone who comes to him.

A couple of months later we had to go on tour, but now that I had found the Lord it was different. No longer did I want to tour alone, I wanted Yvonne with me all the time. It wasn't that I was frightened of being tempted, because the Lord had healed that part of my life, I now wanted Yvonne with me because I loved her and wanted to make up for all those lost years.

It was strange but wonderful that tour, now that I had the Lord with me I looked at everything differently. No longer did I want to run around discos, instead I wanted to be with Yvonne, and it was wonderful that after the show we could go out for meals together, and share our life together, instead of her being at one end of the country and me at the other.

About two weeks into the tour we arrived at Margate.

It was a dismal day with the clouds hanging low over the horizon, that gave the town a feeling of foreboding. But unknown to Yvonne or me it was going to be a day of joy. The evening came and Tommy and I went to our dressing-rooms and got ready to do our show. Before long it was time for Tommy and me to go on stage. We had a full house that night, so there was a feeling of excitement running around backstage. The sound company Wigwam had been in all day setting up their equipment, and as I was now a born-again Christian they were more like brothers to me than just a company we employed. Tommy and I went on stage and did well. When we came off Yvonne was waiting for me.

'I must see Mike Spratt,' she said, very determined.

Now I knew that the only possible reason Yvonne would want to see Mike would be to talk about God. But what Yvonne didn't realise was that when a touring show has finished, it is then that the real work begins. The backstage boys have to pull down all the lights and sound, load them in trucks and then set off to wherever the next show is. The pulling down of the equipment can take anywhere from one to three hours depending on the size of a rig they are using, and I have to tell you that Tommy and I used a big rig. I explained this to Yvonne, but she was adamant. She had to see him now, she said. Now I wasn't about to get in the way of the Lord. The audience had already gone, so I went out into the auditorium and found Mike pulling some gear down.

'Mike,' I said, 'Yvonne wants to see you, I think she wants to talk about the Lord.'

He stared at me with a hopeless look in his eyes.

'I haven't time at the minute, Bob,' he replied. 'I have to get all this gear out.'

'Never mind the gear, Mike,' I said. 'It's your duty to God.'

He looked at me and smiled. 'You're right.'

And we both set off for the dressing-room to see

Yvonne. Mike asked Yvonne what she wanted to see him about, but she said she wanted to see him on her own, privately. The dressing-room by this time was full with people, some visiting, some taking things out, some just hanging around, it was chaotic. So Yvonne and Mike went off together in search of a quiet room.

They were gone for about half an hour, but when Yvonne walked back into my room, it was the most wonderful sight I have ever seen. She was literally glowing with the Holy Spirit. She had been born-again. I looked at her and said, 'You've just found God, haven't you, Yvonne?'

She just smiled and nodded. I was full of questions.

'Now you know the truth, don't you, Yvonne?' I asked, my enthusiasm running at an all-time high.

'Oh, yes,' she replied, her eyes nearly closing.

'How do you feel, Yvonne?' I asked.

She looked at me with a patience that I had not seen in her before.

'All I know, Bob,' she said, 'is that God is very real.'

I could tell that I was asking too many questions, and that she wanted to be quiet and not have the feeling of the Holy Spirit inside her disturbed with my questions. I didn't ask any more, but it was murder for me because I wanted to jump for joy. Now that we were both Christians we would live together for an eternity. It's a wonderful God that we have! Not only, in one sense, had he given me eternal life but, in another sense, he had now given Yvonne to be my 'eternal' wife. Now no longer did she think it was a fad, because now she knew the truth. Now we could walk our journey with Christ together.

Something else happened that night that Yvonne and I have chuckled at ever since. When the Lord came into Yvonne's life and saved her, she was so overcome that with tears of joy running down her face she hugged Mike, and he hugged her back, they were now brothers in

Christ. Just at the moment they were hugging, the door of the tiny dressing-room burst open and in walked one of the crew members who wasn't a Christian. I can just imagine what was running through his mind. There were Bobby Ball's wife and Mike Spratt hugging each other, in a dressing-room hidden away at the back of the theatre. He lowered his eyes and backed out of the dressing-room. I'll bet before long a rumour was running around the theatre that Yvonne and Mike Spratt were having an affair, and that poor Bobby Ball knew nothing about it. Well, I did, and it was the best type of affair she could have.

Before becoming a Christian I hadn't really believed in the Devil, because I hadn't truly believed in the Lord so how could I believe in the Devil? But I have to tell you he's real. After Yvonne and I became Christians the Devil must have realised that he had lost two good disciples, because he decided to persecute us. He started to do things to us that if the Lord hadn't been with us would have cracked us up. Nobody fully understands what we went through, but it was hell. But we praise the Lord, because it just proves how much the Lord loved us for the Devil to attack us the way that he did.

I feel that I have to tell you the story of Yvonne and the Lord's strength in case anybody who reads this book is going through the same thing, and perhaps it will help them.

Yvonne is an epileptic, and about twelve months before I became a Christian Yvonne's fits began to get a little worse. She has never been what I call a bad epileptic, maybe having one major fit a year, but now she started having two or three. She has had them since she was a child and as she grew up she started to ignore them and in the back of her mind she wouldn't admit to having them, because to her it was a stigma. Her fits made her feel different from other people, which of course she is not, and neither is any other epileptic. I knew Yvonne

was an epileptic before I married her, and she was terrified that once I found out I would walk away from her,
but I have a niece who is a bad epileptic, so it didn't
bother me in the least. In fact I think that the govern-
ment should launch a campaign on epilepsy so that everyone can see that these people are normal human beings
who happen to have an ailment and not a contagious
disease. It is a crying shame that people are not given
more information about epilepsy, and then perhaps the
general public would understand that these people are
not social lepers, which they quite often feel. I love my
wife with all my heart for all that she is, and that
includes her epilepsy.

Yvonne hadn't take any medication for many years, so
as her fits started to get worse I talked her into seeing a
private doctor about them. She reluctantly agreed and
off we went to see him. He examined her and prescribed
some tablets that were supposed to control her epilepsy.
They did! But the side effects were horrendous. (Please
remember, dear reader, I hadn't become a Christian yet,
if I had I would have prayed to God for help instead of
trying to go it alone.) Over the next twelve months
Yvonne started to change, but it happened so slowly that
I didn't even notice. To tell you the truth, I don't know
whether I would have noticed anyway, because at that
time I was too interested in my own career. She began
to become very withdrawn, and started to lose weight.
She had also been using sleeping tablets for quite a while,
and these made her quite zombified. When you live with
someone, you are usually the last to notice things,
because change seems to creep up on you slowly, and
then it is accepted as a normal way of living. This is what
happened to Yvonne and me. Yvonne was very ill, but
somehow she managed to hide it from me. She told me
later that she hid her feelings from me because she
thought I had enough on my mind without having her to
worry about. I couldn't tell what was going on in

Yvonne's mind at that time in our lives but I started to notice her weight loss. She was losing it drastically, so I started to nag her about it, saying that she must eat more, and she promised she would, but of course she didn't. When we went out for a meal she would eat only so much and then put her serviette over her plate so that no one would notice how little she had eaten.

During this time the press had started to slate Tom and me. Anything we did on TV, good or bad, they slated it. Even live performances were not safe from them. We went to a club in the Midlands and one newspaper sent a reporter to see us. He didn't introduce himself to us but just sat in the audience to watch our act. That night we got a full standing ovation for about four minutes. We stormed them. But the reporter didn't report that. The next day in the newspaper it said that we were the worst act that the reporter had seen (or words to that effect). He had just reported what he thought of the act and failed to mention what 99 per cent of the audience had thought. Another time Tom and I were doing the London Palladium in a lavish pantomime. There were lots of other stars on the bill with us, and the box office had already taken £300,000 in one week of opening. I think that is still a record today. Over £1 million had been spent on the sets (so the promoter said, and who are we to disbelieve him) so it looked as if the show was going to be a success before we even opened. It was one of the most spectacular shows Tommy and I have ever been in, and we have been in quite a few. On the opening night the show was terrific, everyone seemed pleased with how the show had gone. But in the audience was one man who was a leading critic for a top newspaper. The next day when the newspaper came out he had given us the biggest blasting possible. He criticised the sets, he criticised the performers, in fact I don't think there was anything he didn't criticise. But the truth of the story (and not a lot of people know this) is that he was asleep from the beginning of the panto to the end. The reason I know it is true is because Yvonne was sitting opposite him across the aisle, and watched him all night. He didn't even see the panto. This was the type of thing Tom and I were going through at that time. To be truthful I don't know exactly what a critic does except criticise things, which is a sad job really. I think that no one should criticise what they can't do themselves, because if they could do the job they are criticising they wouldn't be a critic in the first place.

Another great disappointment we suffered was at the hands of our own profession. I had only been a Christian for a few months when we were asked if we would do the cabaret for the Water Rats' ball. Allow me to explain for those people who don't know who the Water Rats are. They are a charity organisation made up of show business people who do some wonderful work. It is a closed society and one has to be approached before one is allowed to join. Both Tommy and I had always wanted to join so it was quite an honour for us when we were asked to be the cabaret at their annual ball. It was a very sophisticated affair, with all the gentlemen in bow ties and all the ladies in ballgowns. As the day got closer both Tommy and I got very excited. We weren't getting paid, but nevertheless we put our own orchestra in at our own expense. After all, who knows, we thought to ourselves, if we go down really well the Water Rats may ask us to join. I will never forget that night as long as I live. The ball was being held at the Grosvenor Hotel, so Tommy and I had to change in one of the bedrooms. When it came time for us to go on stage we were a bundle of nerves. The band played our opening music and we were on. I looked out into the audience and saw all the faces I had seen many times on TV and from billboards. It felt quite an honour to be performing in front of our fellow performers. What happened after that became a nightmare. None of our fellow performers laughed. We were

dying, going down like a lead balloon. I couldn't understand and still don't to this day how members of a profession could watch a fellow member of the same
profession die like we did. It's not as if they were paying
us, we were doing it for charity, we were doing it for
them. We tried to get through the act but it got more
difficult as we went on. I can still see certain faces as
they looked at us as if we were a disease. By the time we
had got three-quarters through the act, the audience of
our fellow performers were talking louder than us.
Eventually we came off and made our way back to the
changing room. Neither Tommy nor I spoke, we were
too heartbroken. How could this happen? How could an
artiste not clap his fellow artiste? It was something that
was alien to Tommy and me. We had always thought
that show business was a family. Well, if it is, then that
night proved that Tommy and I weren't part of it. I have
only written this so that if a Water Rat reads it, they
will realise that it is very difficult to work to one's own
kind, and that every performer needs as much help as he
or she can get.

Meanwhile Yvonne was steadily getting worse. The
Devil was having a wonderful time with our lives. One
day Yvonne admitted to me that she was feeling very
depressed, so I said we would go back to the doctor's.
When we got there Yvonne told the doctor her symptoms.
What blew my mind was that he had to look it up in a
book to see what the side-effects of the tablets were that
he had prescribed for her. When he told us we couldn't
believe our ears. He said that the side-effects were
depression and weight loss. I told him in no uncertain
terms that I was taking her off the tablets because we
were better off when she wasn't on them. He then dropped
the bombshell. He told us that it was impossible to stop
taking the tablets at once otherwise Yvonne would suffer
fit after fit and she could end up in hospital with brain
damage. We sat there not knowing what to do. I felt

that if the doctor had only told us the side-effects before Yvonne had started to take the tablets, I wouldn't have pushed her into taking them. Now I felt I had changed Yvonne from a woman who laughed a lot into a woman who was living in a twilight world.

The doctor then told us that the only way for Yvonne to stop the tablets was to come off them gradually. (She still takes tablets, but these are very mild compared to the ones she had to come off.) We decided that's what we were going to do, so we set off for home with a determination to get Yvonne well again. It was during this period that I found the Lord, and now that I had his help there was nothing we couldn't do.

That season, Tommy and I were working at Paignton in Devon, and by this time we had weaned Yvonne off the tablets. So when season time came around I set off for Paignton and Yvonne stayed at home. About three weeks into the season I got a call saying that she had to come down to see me. I knew something was seriously wrong, so I told her to get a taxi there and then and come to me. When she arrived she was in a right state. I have never seen her looking so bad. She was five foot ten and weighed seven stone three. Now that's thin! As I said before, you can live with someone and not notice anything wrong until the last minute, because you are used to your partner looking that way. But now I had noticed. And now I knew that only with the Lord's help could we get her well. I sat her down and told her to tell me all her troubles. She told me that she thought she had anorexia (caused by the tablets she had just come off) and thought she was hooked on sleeping tablets. I asked her how many sleeping tablets she took a night, and she told me four. I couldn't believe what I was hearing. Yvonne at that time took the strongest sleeping tablet on the market, but she had to take four at a time. (By this time Yvonne also had become a Christian, so the situation wasn't hopeless.) I told her that when the evening came she wasn't to take any sleeping tablets, and if she couldn't sleep she wasn't to worry about it because I would stay up all night with her if necessary. How wrong I was! The evening came and Yvonne and I went to bed. We said our good-nights and tried to go to sleep. After about an hour Yvonne sat up in bed scratching every part of her body. She was having withdrawal symptoms. She was crying and saying that her body was driving her crazy. I felt hopeless, all I could do was sit there with my arms around her and love her. I knew then that this was going to be a long journey, but I also knew that we would succeed. I gave Yvonne a couple of sleeping tablets because I couldn't bear to watch her go through the agony any longer and told her that we would work things out in the morning.

Morning came and the Lord had given me an answer. I told Yvonne that we would wean her off the sleeping tablets, just as we had the epileptic tablets. I told her that one night she could take four, and then the next night take three, and so on until she was no longer depen-dent on them. She agreed with me and that night she took her first steps to recovery. One night I asked her to meet me at the theatre after the show, because we had been invited to go out for a few drinks with friends. For some reason she reluctantly agreed and met me at the end of the show. We met our friends and went across the road to a hotel frequented by all the other acts from the shows in town. We stayed for about an hour, then left. When we got outside Yvonne was as sick as a dog. I asked what she had been drinking, because I was con-vinced that she had had too much to drink, and with her hardly eating anything it wouldn't take a lot to get her drunk. She looked at me with tears in her eyes and explained that she hadn't drunk anything stronger than coffee. She then went on to explain that whenever she left the house she got panic attacks and she felt as if she was choking. She said that she never wanted to leave the house, because it was torture for her to go out. She also said that she wasn't too bad if she was with me but if she was on her own it was one of the most difficult things she had known. Now for someone who has never experienced this, it is very difficult to understand.

We got home and for the first time Yvonne poured her heart out to me. She told me with tears in her eyes all her insecurities, and all her fears. I realised that Yvonne was a strong woman, but over the years I had sapped away that strength, and now she was crying out for some of mine. Sometimes we are quite foolish with the ones we love. I now looked at her and saw a very frightened little girl. This was the mother of my daughter, the woman who now meant more to me than life itself, and I among others had reduced her to this, taking her for granted, a woman who was hooked on sleeping tablets, an anorexic and agoraphobic. I knew now that Yvonne and I had to pray as we had never prayed before. We did! And the Lord started his miraculous work.

That night I lay in bed talking to the Lord, asking what I should do. But unfortunately I got no answers. It's strange, you know, but sometimes when we think that the Lord isn't listening it's at those times that he is working the hardest for us. The next day I set off to the theatre without an answer to my problems, but as the old saying goes, the Lord works in mysterious ways, because on the way there I passed a field and in the middle of it stood a tree, and under the tree was a bench. I stopped the car and looked at the sight in front of my eyes. I knew right away what the answer was. The Lord had answered my prayers. I knew then that Yvonne didn't need any medication, all she needed was the love of the Lord and me. I went home that night feeling very hopeful about the future. I no longer cared about my career or anything else for that matter, all that mattered was Yvonne. She had taken over my life, and that's how I wanted it. I told her about the tree in the field I had found, and then I told her that if she felt up to it we would take it day by day. I told her we must have a plan, and the plan was that we would stay in one day, and the next day we would go and sit under the tree for an hour. We would slowly build up the time she spent out of the house as we went along. She agreed and with the Lord's help we started on the way to recovery. It wasn't easy. It was one of the hardest things we have ever done. Every other day we would call into a little church opposite to where we were staying and say a few prayers before we set off to sit under our tree. It was strange really, by day we were taking Yvonne's agoraphobia step by step, and her anorexia step by step, and by night her dependency on sleeping tablets step by step. No one really knows what we went through. But with the Lord's help we fought the Devil and won.

Every other day we would sit under our tree, holding hands and praying and slowly but surely she started to get her strength back. After a few weeks she had beaten her dependency on sleeping tablets, so at least now she was getting a proper night's sleep. During the middle of all this something happened to me that even now I find hard to forget. Every season Tommy and I would organise a rock 'n' roll show and all the money would go to a local charity. We had been doing this for years, so I reasoned that this year would be no different. That year a very well-known comedian (sorry but he will remain anonymous) was topping the bill at the theatre in Torquay. As luck would have it I ran into him when I was in a local club. I had gone to the club to discuss holding the charity do in it and he was there. I thought that while I had the chance I would ask him if he would do our charity. I knew him very well so I thought it would be no problem to ask him. I walked over to him and tapped him on the shoulder. I wasn't prepared for what greeted me. He turned around and looked at me as if he hated me. I said my hellos and then asked him if he would do the charity. He came closer to me and stood so that we were nose to nose. He was a big star and he usually had a few bodyguards with him; tonight was no exception. They were all just behind him waiting for him to do something. He must have thought he was intimidating me. But he was wrong. I began to feel the Devil rising up inside me. He told me with hate in his eyes that I would be the last person he would do a charity for. I asked him why and he told me that he didn't like me and then asked me what was I going to do about it. I felt the Devil rise to his full force inside me. I wanted to knock him out there and then, just to show his bodyguards that he wasn't that tough and neither were they, but something stopped me. I thought of Jesus, I thought how he would act in this situation. I said I was sorry that he didn't like me and that if I had done anything to him in the past I hoped that he could find it in his heart to forgive me. I then turned on my heel and walked away.

I stayed a little longer at the club to sort out the arrangements for the charity and then I went home. I felt strange, inside the Devil was telling me that I was a coward, and that I should have beaten him up, but deep in my heart I knew that I had done the right thing. I was now a Christian and I had just done what the Lord would have wanted me to do. I told the Devil to go away in no uncertain terms and when I told Yvonne later she said that now I was a real man. She knew that before I had found the Lord I would have hit him, but now the Lord had taught me that violence belonged to the Devil and it had no place in my life any more.

He didn't come to the charity and continued to avoid me. And then when the season was almost at an end I saw him again in the club. I had my back to him and was talking to some of my family when I felt a tap on my shoulder. I turned round and it was him. He asked me how the charity had gone down. Well . . . it was a very strange situation, here was this man who a few weeks ago had arrogantly intimidated me, now asking me humbly how the charity had gone. I took him by the arm and led him away from the crowds of people. I'll bet he thought I was taking him to one side to hit him. But that was the furthest thing from my mind. I asked him what the problem was, and he told me that he had noticed I was a different man from the one I used to be. I replied I knew that because I had God looking after me. I could tell by looking in his eyes that he didn't know what that statement meant, so I decided to ask him what his reasons were for disliking me. He replied that years before I had bitten his ear in a club in London and that I had made it bleed.

'Oh! Is that all!' I said.

And then I proceeded to put him on the floor and playfully pretended to bite his ear, only this time being careful not to draw blood. We laughed, and that night we walked away with a new respect for one another. But if he reads this book I would like to meet him again to explain to him how the power of the Lord changed me from an ear-biting mongrel to someone who respects people. Also I would like to meet him again because inside he isn't truly happy, and I know through experience, because I was like him. Only the Lord can truly help him.

By now the season was nearing an end, and Yvonne's ailments were definitely on the mend. We had got over her addiction to sleeping tablets and by this time she was sleeping soundly without them. We were winning the battle with her agoraphobia because now she had got to the stage where she could go out with me and not get any panic attacks. She was still painfully thin, but I knew that she could only get better. One only has to think about the type of life Yvonne had before we were Christians; she had a husband she couldn't fully trust, she never knew when I was coming home and she never knew when I was going to explode in a fit of anger. It's no wonder that she was an emotional wreck. But every day through the season we prayed and slowly but surely she started to get well.

We arrived home after the summer season feeling quite emotionally battered, but at least Yvonne and I were winning our battle with the Devil. One day when we were shopping in the village I stayed in the car while Yvonne did some shopping. I seemed to have been waiting only a few moments before she came back. I asked her what was wrong and she told me that everything was fine and that she had done her shopping. I thought no more of it until the following week when we went into the village again. All through the time Yvonne was ill she had tried to hide her emotions from me, but this time I was suspicious of her lightning shopping trips. So the next time we went to the shops I followed her. I was amazed to see her actually run around the shops as if the Devil himself was after her. She didn't know I was watching her so when she got back to the car I was already waiting. I asked why she had run round the shops instead of walking, explaining to her that I had been watching. She then admitted that she still got panic attacks, and that she was running because there was no way she could have walked round. I told her that the next time she went to the shops I was going to try something. The following week came and we set off to the village. I parked my car at the top of the high street and told Yvonne that I would be watching her as she did her shopping. I was parked on double yellow lines and I could tell that inside Yvonne was panicking, because she used this and many other excuses not to go.

'You can't park here,' she said, 'you might get a ticket.'

I told her not to worry and after much persuasion she set off down the high street to do her shopping. Slowly I followed her in the car, and every time she started to run I would shout, 'Walk, Yvonne.' This seemed to have the desired effect, because she was actually walking. We did

this quite a few times. Yvonne said it was all right if
somebody else was there, but there was no way she could
do it on her own. She was fine if she went shopping with
our Mavis or if I was following her in the car, but otherwise she stayed in the house.

This went on for a couple of months and then one morning I got up and Yvonne wasn't in the house. I wasn't
unduly worried because I thought she must have gone
out with our Mavis. So I made myself a cup of tea and
settled down to read my papers. I had only sat down for
a couple of minutes or so when a taxi pulled up. Yvonne
got out of it alone, paid the taxi and came into the house.
Her face was blooming, she looked like the cat who had
got the cream. She sat me down and told me that she had
just walked round the village on her own. She looked so
proud of herself, and to tell you the truth, I was proud of
her too. She then told me that she had got up that morning feeling very down, and then she prayed to the Lord
and something told her to go to the village on her own.
She said it took a lot of courage, but nevertheless she did
it. When she got there, she started to feel the old panic
attacks coming on but she managed to control them. She
finished her story and sat back glowing. She knew she
had taken a step forward. I really believe that instead of
our Mavis or me walking with Yvonne, the Lord was
doing it that morning. He had said to himself that
Yvonne had taken enough from the Devil and now he
was taking over. From that morning Yvonne started to
get better and better. Over the next two years she got
stronger and stronger until now she is back to her normal
weight, and no longer has panic attacks. Once more she
is the one I lean on and through God's grace she is a
stronger woman now than she has ever been all her life.

Becoming a Christian and finding the Lord (it's a funny
statement, that, isn't it, 'finding the Lord', he has never
been lost) is the best thing that has ever happened to me.
He has done so much within my life, reshaping me and

rebuilding me. He has also introduced me to other Christians who have become close friends, Ray Bevan, Chris Gidney, Mike Spratt and Ken Woodward, Dave Bemment, Max Wigley and of course their families. I don't mean to miss anyone out but I have found friends through the Lord too numerous to mention. At one time I thought I would have found these people boring, but now I find them the most interesting people I know. They don't want to be friends with you for what you are, or for what you can do, but because they are brothers in Christ. I know that these people would never let me down or talk behind my back, but the most important thing is that I know I could trust them with my life. Thank you, each and every one of you.

Not long after Yvonne and I had become Christians I decided I wanted to be baptised. I felt that I wanted to make some sort of commitment to the Lord (I didn't yet realise that I had made the biggest commitment by asking him into my life). I asked Yvonne if she would like to join me in being baptised. She asked me what it would involve, so I said I would ask our local church, Heywood Baptist, about it (this is the church Mike Spratt attends). I asked Mike if it would be possible for Yvonne and me to be baptised in his church, and he said it would. I then asked him all about what happens when one is baptised. He told me that we would need some old jeans and a change of clothes for after the baptism and explained certain other things that happen. I relayed what he had told me to Yvonne, she agreed and we set a date to be baptised. I will never forget that day as long as I live. We set out for the church with our change of clothes under our arms wondering what was going to happen. When we arrived Mike Hook, who was the minister, took us into a back room and started to explain. I could see Yvonne slowly turning white. Mike told us that he would call our names out, and we would have to go up to the front of the church, stand in front of the microphone and

tell the congregation how we came to know the Lord.
Then we would have to make our way down to where we
were to be baptised, get into the water, where two men
would lay us back and submerge us fully under water.
Yvonne panicked as (A) there was no way she would be
able to stand in front of a lot of people and talk; and (B)
she couldn't swim, so to have her head put under water
would be agony for her. I was all right because I can
swim and it didn't bother me talking, that is one of my
best features, I can bore people to death talking. But at
that moment Yvonne was the problem. She started to
really panic. Mike Hook said not to worry because everything would be all right.

We sat down in the church and started to pray. It's a
funny thing but sometimes even as Christians each and
every one of us finds it difficult to give everything to the
Lord. But luckily for us that night we did. Yvonne and
I just sat there praying like mad as Mike Hook began
calling out names of people who were being baptised.
Yvonne was gripping my hand and I thought that any
moment she was going to break it off. Suddenly my name
was called. I looked at Yvonne as she sat there, and she
looked so vulnerable, but before I knew it I was on my
way to the front of the church. If you ask me to explain
fully what happened next I can't, all I can say is while I
was on my way down the Holy Spirit filled me, I felt I
was going to burst. The tears started to stream down my
face, and it felt as if I was being reborn-again. By the
time I reached the microphone I couldn't speak for the
tears flowing down my face. I didn't want to speak, I just
wanted to stay with this overwhelming feeling of peace
that the Lord was giving me. Mike handed me the mike
and I just gave it back to him. There was no need for me
to talk about the Lord, the people there could see him
within me. I then walked into the water and was baptised
in the name of the Lord. After I had been baptised I
looked over to where Yvonne was sitting and she looked

like a small child who had been left out in the cold. Suddenly her name was called out and without any hesitation she immediately made her way to the front of the church, got hold of the microphone and then proceeded to talk about the Lord for ten minutes. She told stories that had the congregation in fits of laughter, there was no stopping her. I just stood there in the water watching her open-mouthed. Was this my wife who a few moments ago was a dithering wreck? She finished talking and walked straight into the water beside me and got baptised. It didn't seem to bother her in the least when her head was ducked underwater. With tears of joy running down our faces we held each other. We both knew now that no matter what tribulations and troubles the Devil threw at us we would always be strong enough because the Lord was well and truly with us. Now the Lord works in mysterious ways, he uses each person in his own way. Looking back on our baptism, the Lord had reversed the roles with Yvonne and me, he had given me the quietness and meekness of the Holy Spirit, and he had given Yvonne the confidence and the boldness of the Holy Spirit. Because on that day that is exactly what we needed. It's quite true that the Lord provides! And he also provides miracles! Yes, you read it right, *miracles*. But more about that in the next chapter.

9

Miracles never cease

Today, after many years of illness, Yvonne is back to normal. She is the backbone of the family once more. Her panic attacks have been replaced by a gentle confidence, and I am thinking of entering her for the Olympics for eating. Her weight is now normal, and I thank God for the miracle that he performed with Yvonne. He gave me back my wife.

Talking of miracles, not so long ago I felt a lump on one of my testicles (if that word upsets anyone, then I am sorry, but I don't know another word for them). Anyway I told Yvonne about it and she said she would take a look. She did and felt the lump I had been talking about. She immediately said she was going to ring the doctor. I started to make excuses at this point. I know to a lot of people that have seen me on TV I may seem rather brash and loud, but when it comes to personal matters such as this I am very shy. (In fact I think Yvonne has only seen me naked about a dozen times during the whole of our marriage. She actually takes the mickey out of me because of it. I call it decency, she calls it stupidity, well, maybe she's right.) Anyway she talked me into it and arranged for us to go and see the doctor the next day. We both realised that if anything was wrong it was going to be awkward because the day after visiting the doctor we would be setting off for Great Yarmouth to start a summer season. But nevertheless, we reasoned, let's get over one hurdle first. We arrived at the doctor's and he asked me into his surgery. This was going to be the first time that a man had examined my most private parts. I have never felt so embarrassed in my life. I know it's silly! But I couldn't help it. So I tried to make jokes all the time to cover my embarrassment.

The doctor never gave me even a glimmer of a smile. It was getting more embarrassing by the moment. Eventually he asked me to dress and told me that he had found a lump that shouldn't be there. I have to be honest, this worried me. He said that he would like me to go to a specialist as soon as possible. I told him this was impossible as I was going to Yarmouth the next day. He then made an appointment for me to see a doctor in Yarmouth and told me that I had to go as soon as I got there. I came straight out with the million-dollar question and asked him if it was malignant or not. He told me he didn't know until further tests had been done. Yvonne and I went home that day feeling very worried but for some reason we kept our fears from one another.

The next day we arrived in Great Yarmouth and went to the doctor's there. Once again I had to go through the embarrassment of being examined. When he had finished he told us that he had found the growth and he would like me to go to a specialist that dealt with this kind of thing. Now he had confirmed my worst fears, I did have a growth, and the doctors seemed concerned about it. I tried to laugh it off with Yvonne but I could see she was worried. We prayed a lot during this period. The doctor made an appointment with the specialist for the week after, and I have to tell you that was the longest week of my life. But as there is no stopping time the day soon came round for me to go. Yvonne and I said our prayers before we set off and trusted in the Lord. We arrived at

the specialist's and before I knew where I was I was once
more on the couch being examined.

He felt around for quite a while and then said he had
found the growth and now he would like me to go and
have a scan to see what kind of growth he was dealing
with.

We were devastated. We imagined the worst scenario,
but funnily enough we still kept our fears to ourselves.
The specialist arranged for us to go to the hospital the
following day so we didn't have long to wait. When we
arrived both Yvonne and I were a bag of nerves. They
took us down a long corridor towards the scanning area,
then they asked us to sit down and said our names would
be called shortly. Yvonne and I sat down and immediately held hands, we didn't speak but just smiled weakly
at each other. Eventually my name was called and I had
to go into this room where they gave me a sort of dressing-
gown to put on. It was the kind of dressing-gown that
covers the front but allows one's rear quarters to get cold
very rapidly. Then I was sent into another room where
all the scanning machinery was. In the room were a man
and a woman. Oh no, not a woman! Now a woman was
going to see my most prized possessions. This was my
worst nightmare coming true. The doctor asked me to sit
down, which I did, and then he proceeded to put a type
of jelly all over me. This was getting worse! Luckily the
nurse was over the other side of the room, so at least
I had that in my favour. He then started to take his
photographs. I could see the doctor start to frown, and I
thought that he was worried. He was! But he was worrying about something totally different from me. He looked
worried because he couldn't find the lump on the screen.
He kept taking different pictures, but still he couldn't
see anything. Eventually he gave up on this and started
to try to find it manually. Now what he did to me I
wouldn't wish on any man. Remember I didn't know that
he couldn't find anything, so what with the worried look

on his face, and with his pulling and shoving, it seemed
to me that he was trying to pull the growth out manually.
At long last he stopped his 'wrestling' with me and went
back to taking pictures. After a while he called his nurse
over to take a look. How embarrassing. There I lay like
a chicken ready for Christmas and these two people were
discussing the most personal part of my anatomy.

'Look at this, nurse,' he said, 'it's a perfect specimen.
It's actually textbook material.'

Now I know that they were talking medically and that
it was nothing to them, but they were talking about me,
and more importantly, something that was very private
to me. Eventually, after much probing, he told me that
he couldn't find anything wrong with me.

'In fact,' he said, 'it is most puzzling, because I can't
find any sign of a growth, even my pictures didn't show
one.'

I told him that three doctors had felt the growth. He
said that he understood this, which is what made it a
mystery to him, because the specialist who sent me was
never wrong about his diagnosis of things like this. He
then told me to get dressed because I was fine. I left the
room in a state of confusion. Three doctors had found a
growth, even a specialist, and now there wasn't one, not
even a trace of there ever having been one. Yvonne was
outside in the waiting-room, and when I went to collect
her, she looked at me with hope in her eyes. I told her
what the doctor had said and then she just said, 'My
prayers have been answered.'

My confusion left me, I then knew that she had been
praying for me and that the Lord had answered. What I
didn't know until later was that Yvonne had phoned Ray
Bevan and a few more of our Christian friends and they
had all been praying for me. The Lord had performed a
miracle. He had taken away the growth. Praise the Lord!
It is quite impossible for someone who is not a Christian
to understand this, because they do not know the power

of the Lord. Only when we have had our sins forgiven
and let the Lord into our lives, can we truly begin to see
the greatness of our Father.

As I have said before, it wasn't until I became a Christian that I really believed in the Devil. But now I know
that he is real. When I became a Christian he lost a very
good disciple and he wasn't happy. When one becomes a
follower of Jesus Christ, one automatically turns one's
back on the Devil and the Devil doesn't like it, so he
starts to attack. One suddenly sees the Devil for what he
really is, a weak insipid creature who is only happy when
one is sinning. The Devil is a very conniving creature,
and what we take as natural human behaviour – anger,
frustration, gossip, greed, putting ourselves first – is not
natural at all. I am here to tell you, friend, that these
works are the work of the Devil. We are all guilty of
them, even Christians. But when we recognise that these
temptations are the work of the Devil, then we see him
for what he really is. Don't get me wrong, I am not saying
that being a Christian one is safe from these temptations,
quite the contrary, the Devil attacks us more.

Allow me to tell you a little story. When I first became
a Christian I was full of the Lord and wanted to tell the
world about it, so I started to do some gospel shows, just
to tell people what wonderful work the Lord had done in
my life. Every time I was going to set out to do them,
Yvonne and I would have a row over some trivial thing.
Yvonne would then sit me down and explain to me that
the Devil was making us argue because I was going to
talk about the Lord. Once I had fully understood this the
Devil stopped making us argue, he knew it would be a
waste of time because I would just send him away in the
name of the Lord. What I am trying to say is that even
though one is a Christian the Devil still continues to
battle for our soul, and sometimes one can slip. But the
Lord is always there to pick us up. Once we accept Jesus
into our lives the Lord promises that he will never leave

us. The Lord doesn't break his promises, only man does that, through the Devil. I love the Lord with all my heart and I bless the day that he saved me. The greatest day of my life was when I found the Lord and kicked the Devil in the face!

During my time with the Lord he has blessed me and done many great miracles for me. Two years ago something wonderful happened in my life, my daughter became a Christian. It was my birthday and we had gone for a meal first and then on to a pub. Now I know that some Christians will say that I shouldn't be in a pub, well, I have this to say to them. They should follow the example of Jesus! Because those are the types of places that Jesus would visit today and I don't just mean pubs. I mean discos, red light districts, drug areas, anywhere that the Devil resides. I have even thought, should I be in show business with its pockets of homosexuality, alcoholism and adultery? Should I be among this? Will I be tempted? Well, I found that the answer was yes! Undoubtedly yes! I realised that the Devil would tempt me but I knew that the Lord would be protecting me against all these things. So I truly believe that my place is in show business, until such time as the Lord decides otherwise. I am not talking about Christians walking into pubs and such to knock people over the heads with the Bible, but of a more gentle approach that Jesus would have followed. Believe me, if one is walking with the Lord he will shine through, and when one gently mentions in conversation that one is a follower of the Lord, people will begin to ask questions. Because there is a hunger out there that needs to be satisfied. And who knows that somewhere in a sin-filled room someone may be saved through a statement such as 'I am a born-again Christian!'

As I was saying before, the family had taken me out to celebrate my birthday and we had ended up in a pub. As usual I was talking to my children about God, which

they found very interesting, when suddenly my daughter
said she was going to the toilet. She had been quiet all
night, so my Yvonne went with her. I carried on talking
to the boys. Eventually the ladies came back, and when
I saw my Joanne I knew, tears were streaming down her
face, and she was full of the Holy Spirit.

'You have found him, haven't you?' I said.

She just nodded, because she was too full of the Holy
Spirit to talk. Yvonne told me later that when they got
into the ladies Joanne told her that she had been having
these feelings about the Lord for quite a while. So Yvonne
took her hands and prayed over her. Then the Holy Spirit
came in and blessed her. She had walked into the toilets
alone and came out walking with God! It's strange but
the Lord will follow anyone anywhere to give them eternal life. One only has to ask! Isn't he a wonderful God!

My Joanne is now a committed Christian with very
strong beliefs, every day I can see her growing, and now
she is getting a hunger for more in her Christian life.
What is marvellous is that she teaches me things. God
has truly blessed her with a wisdom beyond her years. I
continually pray for the boys, hoping that some day they
too will see the truth. They are always asking questions,
so who knows. Our Robert has asked me to take him with
me when I go down to Newport to do a gospel show later
this year. So who knows, by the time this book is pub-
lished he may have been saved. We will have to wait and
see.

I've said a lot about my family but you may be wondering what my partner Tommy was thinking all this time.
To get the story from the horse's mouth, so to speak, I
recently asked Tommy and his lady Hazel what they
thought about me when I became a Christian. I sat them
down and interviewed them. The reason I did this was
because we had never discussed my Christianity deeply
before, and I decided that it was about time. This is how
the two interviews went.

Hazel's interview

BOB When was the first time I told you that I had become a Christian?

HAZEL I remember exactly the first time you told me. We were on a plane going to the Middle East. And you said, 'Has Tommy told you that I have become a born-again Christian?' And I said, 'So I believe.'

BOB And what did you think?

HAZEL I honestly thought, oh, it's one of his hair-brained schemes, he's found something else to do. Give him a couple of weeks or so and he will get it out of his system. He'll be fine. That was the initial thought. But then again I didn't even think enough about it because I didn't understand what it was all about. Well, maybe I didn't want to understand it.

BOB Did you see a change in me?

HAZEL Yes, a drastic change.

BOB At the beginning, or over a space of time?

HAZEL Over a space of time, maybe not initially, but then again I wasn't looking for a change. Not initially, no, but over a period of years, definitely yes!

BOB And what kind of change did you see?

HAZEL A lot more peace within yourself, not as aggressive, just completely different, as if you had found sort of an inner peace.

BOB Did it intrigue you?

HAZEL Yes! It amazed me. That you had become this different person. That suddenly you had become this born-again Christian. What had happened in your life? If you remember I sat down and asked you once. I said, tell me what happened, did someone talk to you inside and tell you, you should not be this way? And you tried to explain to me, but I think if one doesn't want to understand, or can't be bothered to understand, then one can't be bothered, can they? But I did see a drastic change in you, yes.

BOB After three or four years did you then think that my faith was for real?

HAZEL Yes. I became used to you being this different person. In the beginning I used to think, I hope he doesn't go back to being the other person again and he stays this way. So, yes, for the first two or three years one was waiting, thinking if there was a crisis going to happen he's going to go back to what he was. And then one gets used to it. One gets used to someone being a certain way. The greatest thing is you have got better and better. You seem to get more peaceful all the time.

Tom's interview

BOB What did you first think when I told you I had become a Christian?

TOM To be honest, I thought you were a crackpot. I couldn't believe it. I thought this is a nonsense, this, it's a cop-out, that's what I thought it was. I thought, he's told me now that he's been forgiven for his sins. Well, I've got to be honest, there's no way, I thought, he's been forgiven for having been the way that he was. And that is exactly what I thought from the very beginning.

BOB Did it annoy you in any way?

TOM No! It never bothered me either way, like when I went playing golf with some of the lads they used to ask me, 'What's up with Bobby and all this Christian rubbish?' And I used to say, 'Hey, it's his own thing.' And that's about how much it affected me.

BOB Did you ever say to yourself, well, it may be good for him but it's definitely not for me?

TOM No, I don't think I ever did. Hazel and I discussed it. I've said to her before today, 'What do you think about all this Christianity and Bobby?' and we both thought it was a fad and that you would soon go back to being the old Bobby Ball. But the answer to your question is no, I never did.

BOB Did you see a change in me?

TOM No! Not at first! But I will say for the last four or five years I have seen a big change. But then again when you first became a Christian I wasn't looking for it. I was too busy waiting for you to slip up. And of course in the early days when you first became a Christian you were still swearing within the act, so I thought to myself there's no way that this man can be a Christian. And then more of a peacefulness came about you. Which I quite liked. And I think I've been thinking to myself, 'Well, whatever he's got it's great! Because he certainly is a changed person, and maybe I want some of it.' Maybe I was a bit jealous of what you had, I don't know. I mean, in the early days I suppose you were learning but now you are a different person. You are more peaceful still. It's like chalk and cheese between what you used to be and what you are now.

BOB I remember you once said to me that you were a Christian, and I said you weren't. How did that make you feel?

TOM Confused. Yes, it really confused me. Because in my eyes then I thought I was a Christian. I had always gone to church as a child and I was brought up to believe in God. As I got older I always believed that there was something, but I suppose like a lot of people I thought I would be able to sort it out when I was dead. But of course now I know the truth.

BOB Do you remember the first time you asked me a question about God? Was it to try and trip me up or was it because you were genuinely interested?

TOM Yes, I remember the first question I asked you, and no, I wasn't trying to trip you up. I wanted an answer to my question. I remember I was sitting in a doctor's surgery and I was reading a magazine and it said in the magazine, 'If a murderer met God, would God forgive him?' This question intrigued me, so I thought, I know the person to ask. Which was you. You then told

me that if the murderer asked for the Lord's forgiveness then he would be forgiven. At that time I couldn't
understand.

BOB   But you do now?

TOM   Oh, yes!

BOB   And it was through that question you started
      thinking about the Lord.

TOM   Yes, that is when I started to want to know more.

A miracle happened on November 8th 1992. Tommy and
I were working at a club in South Wales. It wasn't very
far from Ray Bevan's church, so my daughter Joanne
decided to have her son Christian dedicated to the Lord.
Ray arranged things, so everything was all planned for
the ceremony to be held on the 8th. About a week before
we were due to go, Yvonne suggested that we asked Tom
and Hazel if they would like to go with us to have their
daughter Kelly dedicated at the same time as Christian.
I suggested this to Tommy and he refused in no uncertain
manner. I decided I had better leave it, so I didn't bother
asking again. But, surprise, surprise, a couple of days
later Tommy asked if it would be possible for me to
arrange it. Would it be possible! This was an answer from
God. I told him there would be no problem, and then
Yvonne phoned Ray Bevan and sorted it out. The day
soon arrived for us all to go to church. It was the first
time Tommy had been to a church like Ray's. The King's
Church in Newport, Gwent is a Holy Spirit-filled church.
It is a wonderful place with blessings in abundance. And
Ray is a wonderful pastor who makes the word of God
understandable for the non-believer. There is great singing of the Lord's praises and wonderful stories told. It
was the type of place that even Tommy could not fail to
be impressed with.

We arrived at the church and Ray took us into his office
and gave us a cup of tea before the service started. He
was marvellous. He was trying to put Tommy and Hazel

at ease, but I could see that Tommy and Hazel were far from comfortable. I could understand it really, there they were surrounded by born-again Christians and not fully understanding what it meant. It's strange but when one comes into the Lord's presence, and one hasn't been forgiven for one's sins, one has a feeling of not belonging, a sort of being an outsider feeling. It is the Devil who creates these feelings, because one is never an outsider to the Lord. The more one sins, the more the Lord cries and wants to forgive. But it is the Devil who tries to stop this by making us feel that we don't belong in church. In fact we belong wherever the Lord is.

Anyway, back to the story of the miracle. After we had drunk our tea Ray led us out into the church to sit down. As we entered a man came forward and hugged Tommy and said, 'Bless you, Tommy.' This threw Tommy totally. If he didn't believe we were all crackpots before, he certainly did now. I saw the look on his face and he didn't know what to do. I just simply smiled to myself, because I knew that the Lord was hitting him on the head. We sat down and before long the whole congregation were singing out the praises of the Lord. I took a sneaky look at Tommy and Hazel and there they were singing out at the top of their voices. After we had finished singing Ray asked us all to step up to the podium while he dedicated the children. It was a wonderful ceremony and one that was well worth waiting for. After Ray had finished dedicating the children he asked us to sit down. He then gave a sermon on forgiveness of sins and coming to the Lord. I could see Tommy listening intently, so I started to pray. Yvonne and I along with a few others had been praying for Tommy and Hazel for weeks. The Lord had already answered part of my prayers by getting them to come. It was a very powerful sermon that Ray preached in layman terms and I could see it was having an effect on Tommy. After Ray had finished he asked people who felt that they wanted to be forgiven for their sins and make a commitment to the Lord to raise their hands. Every head in the church was bowed and I didn't even look at Tommy and Hazel. I was too busy praying. It would be beyond my wildest dreams for Tommy and Hazel to join me and Yvonne on our journey with the Lord. I could hear Ray in the background asking people to raise their hands, when suddenly Yvonne dug me in the ribs. I stopped praying and looked at her wondering what the matter could be. She just looked at me with tears in her eyes, she then nodded over to where Tom and Hazel sat. Their hands were up in the air.

I cannot begin to describe what I felt. It was a tremendous sense of joy. Tears started to run down my face because I knew then that Tommy and Hazel would find the peace that they had been searching so long for. I would no longer be a crackpot to Tommy but a brother. The Lord had truly answered my prayers. Thank you, Lord! Ray then asked the people who had put their hands up to come forward so that they could receive the Holy Spirit. By this time both Yvonne and I were in tears. It was glorious. It is a wonderful thing to see, when someone accepts the Lord into their life. Tommy and Hazel went forward hand in hand and stood before Ray. I could already see a change in them.

After the service we went back to Ray's office for tea, and both Tommy and Hazel were different people. They knew the truth. They had been forgiven and you could actually see the weight that had been lifted off Tommy's shoulders. He now had the 'peace' that he had seen in me. But the good news was he now understood why. The Lord had performed a miracle for me that day. He had saved Tom and Hazel. From now on I knew that our lives would change and so would our careers. There would be no more mood changes or wondering separately where we were heading, we would know and we would be doing it together. When we left the church that day Tommy and Hazel were different. They were at peace with themselves. I know that people in show business will sneer and mock at Tom and me, because I did it myself to other people before I knew the truth, but these people should find out the truth about the Lord before they do. And to tell you the truth, it's all right if they mock, because perhaps some of them will enquire about it and then Tom and I will be able to explain about the wonderful story of our Lord.

Since that day Tommy and Hazel have grown as Christians, and it is wonderful to see. Before Tommy found the Lord he could not say a sentence without a profanity coming from his mouth. Since the minute he walked out of that church that morning he hasn't sworn once, and has said that he doesn't want to. I can tell you from experience that if one swears continually it becomes a habit that is as hard to break as smoking. I know this sounds silly but it is the truth. I know that one can stop for a few days but eventually one will slip up. Tommy hasn't! And it is only through the grace of God that he has been able to do it. About five weeks after he became a Christian we were staying in a hotel in Bristol, and a man came to the bar. After about ten minutes he was swearing his head off. Tommy couldn't take it any more and walked away saying, 'To think I used to swear like that!'

He wasn't decrying the man, it's just that now Tommy finds it offensive, and that's not saying that he's a prude. It's just that a person's view of the world changes when one looks at it through God's eyes.

As you have read, my life has been a series of ups and downs. But since 1986 my life has been on the up. So many wonderful things have happened to me since I found God. I am not talking about material things or career success; but spiritually. I have found a great sense of peace. All I ever want to do now is get closer to the Lord. I know that some people will not understand this, but that's fine, because I do. Tommy and I have never been one of the show business clique (and, oh yes, there is one) and at one time it bothered me. I used to think it was because we spoke in broad northern accents, or because we didn't act as 'stars' should; I don't know. But now it no longer bothers me because I belong to something bigger, a brotherhood in God. Everything seems trivial when one looks at the magnitude of God. It hurts me when I hear everyone blaming the Lord for what is happening in the world. It's not really his fault when *we* are the ones who so often cause pain and suffering, is it?

My life now is much more contented than ever it was before. Yvonne and I live in a sixteenth-century farmhouse high on the hills overlooking the Calderdale Valley, and it is marvellous to get up in the morning and see God's work all around. It is wonderful in the springtime to see the newborn lambs jumping high in the air, full of the life that God has given them. I also have a donkey named Jemima, so with the lambs and donkey I am continually reminded of the story of Jesus. Yes, life is very good to me. I look at Yvonne and to me she gets prettier every day. I know to some people that might sound soppy, but it's the truth, and when I look back on what my life used to be I thank the Lord for all he has done for me, particularly for allowing me to keep my wife. Because I can see now that before I became a Christian it was only through her strength and her love for me that we stayed together. Thank you, Yvonne! We have a love now that is born in heaven. Every day it is wonderful to wake up and see my family around me, and if there is a crisis my whole family, Mavis, Trevor, everyone pulls together. It is wonderful to know that I have been blessed with these people. What is more wonderful is that through show business I could have lost them, by thinking too much of myself, but the Lord has shown me where my priorities are, and I thank him for that. He has shown me that one kiss from my wife is worth a thousand women, because she is kissing me with real love.

Many men think that drinking, womanising, fighting and clawing their way up power mountains is the way that life should be lived. But they are wrong, I know because I have been there. If these people are truly honest with themselves and look deep into their hearts they will see that they are not truly happy, something is missing. The thing that is missing is God, because no one can be truly happy until they have found him. And I say those who have not found the Lord live in hope that when they die God will forgive them for what they have done wrong while they were living. But a man or woman who has found God does not fear death, nor do they just have a vague hope. They have fact! Because God has already forgiven them so that, when they die, they will live with him. (I realise that people will say, 'How do I know this?' Well, I know, because I have found that the Bible is true. Some people will object that the Bible can't be trusted, but I have found it to be completely trustworthy.)

There are other people reading this book who will say that becoming a born-again Christian is taking the easy way out and that God wants us to stand on our own feet. Well, I don't think he does. He says give everything to him and he will help us with all things. Something else many people believe is that to be a Christian all one has to do is good works and go to church and pray. Well, to be a Christian it takes a lot more than that. One has to make a commitment to the Lord, first by asking him to forgive one's sins, and then for him to live within one's life. Allow me to illustrate what I mean.

If you have a bottle and fill it with milk, and you leave just a tiny bit of the old milk in the bottle, then the old milk will curdle the new. That is why we must thoroughly wash the bottle first with the Holy Spirit, before we can pour the milk of God into it.

In other words we must ask the Lord to take away our old life before we can start a new one. We don't have to pray a lot or do as many good deeds as we can or work hard to gain favour with the Lord. The Lord gives his gift of life freely, it is ours to take. We were given it by Jesus dying on the cross. Once we have started our new life with God, praying, good deeds and working come as a natural progression. I know also that people will say that it is easy for me to speak this way because I have a lot of money, so therefore life is easier. Well, I have to destroy the myth that the tabloid press has built up. I have no piles of money! I have to work to pay my mortgage. But I am far happier now than when I was rich. You see, my friend the Lord has taken away my excess. I don't need it. The Lord will provide for my needs. I would sooner have just one drop of the Lord's grace in my life than a whole bank full of money.

The old life that I used to lead of womanising, drinking and fighting seems alien to me now. I can never understand now how anyone could be like that. But the Lord's grace has done that for me. And the good news is that it can happen to anyone. God loves us all!

Well, we've reached the end and I want to thank you for reading this book. I am sorry if it bored you in places, but I got bored sometimes with my life so why shouldn't you be!

Thank you once again, dear reader, but before you close the last page on my innermost thoughts I would like you to read this prayer I wrote for myself. It helps me sometimes, perhaps it can help you.

Prayer for myself

In this world of ever-changing faces, help me to stay on the straight line I was destined to be on.

Help me to try and put right my faults, but to realise that my strengths are gifts.

Help me to be patient with others who are as impatient as myself.

Help me to learn the value of each minute of each day that I have on this earth, that I can bring love and happiness into someone else's life and not just my own.

Teach me to be honest with myself because if I am not honest with myself first, then it is impossible to be honest with others.

Make me slow to speak but quick to listen because others have a point of view too.

Help me to gain a little wisdom as each day goes by because the smallest grain of wisdom is worth all the riches on earth.

Grant me peace and serenity that I may enjoy the days that I have left on earth.

Help me to see the good in others before the bad.

And last of all, help me to be honest in all that I do, and to help others in all that I do, because in spite of all our insecurities and faults we are the children of God and he gave us life.

So I shall try each day to become a better human being and, when my time comes to leave this wonderful world, I can go to God in the knowledge that at least I tried.   Amen.

Afterword

Life after *My Life*

It has been a couple of years now since I finished writing *My Life* and quite a few things have happened to me since then, some good, some bad.

On April 5th 1993 the Lord took my dad. He hadn't been well for a while so, although I was sad to lose him, another part of me was glad that he wouldn't be in any more pain. He was a great man. I know that the word 'great' is thrown around loosely these days, but to me my dad *was* a great man. He taught us so many things and prepared me for the battle of life. I think that without his guidance I would not have been able to handle life the way that I have. Sometimes, late at night when I am alone; he wanders back into my mind and once again it is just as if he is with me. He will always have a place in my heart and I can always look back and think of him as a wonderful father.

On a lighter note I have been presented with my first grand-daughter! I already have two grandsons, Ben and Christian, and they drive me ragged, so it is nice to have a quiet, petite granddaughter, or am I kidding myself? Allow me just two seconds to describe my granddaughter – after all, that is a grandfather's prerogative. She is called Bethany and she is beautiful, with more hair than I have ever seen on a child. At the moment she is always screaming to be fed, but the time will come when I will be able to sit her on my knee and tell her all the stories my father told me.

Last, but by no means least, my partner and friend Tommy is growing every day with Jesus. It is a pleasure to see. He is forever asking me questions about Christianity and reading his Bible. It is wonderful to witness him growing in Christ. I can only praise the Lord for the way he has turned Tommy's life around – but that is the subject of another story!

As for myself and Yvonne, life couldn't be better. I find that I am coming closer to the Lord day by day, and that is all that is important to me. In a way, nothing else matters. As long as I am growing and trying to be the person the Lord would like me to be, then I am happy. I find that since I wrote *My Life* I have found even more peace in my heart and my only ambition left now is to introduce the Lord to as many people as I can. If I can do that then my life will have been complete.

BOBBY BALL
1995